485

THE NEW CHILD

Bhagwan Shree Rajneesh
is now known simply
as Osho.

Osho has explained that
His name is derived
from William James' word
'oceanic' which means
dissolving into the ocean.
Oceanic describes the
experience, He says,
but what about
the experiencer? For that
we use the word 'Osho'.
Later He came to find out
that 'Osho' has also been used
historically in the Far East
meaning
"The Blessed One, on whom
the Sky Showers Flowers."

Published by
Sterling Publishers Private Limited

THE
NEW CHILD

OSHO

Published by Sterling Publishers (India) New Delhi-110 016
Printed at Sona Printers, New Delhi-110 020
Cover design: John Capra

A Sterling Paperback

STERLING PAPERBACKS
An imprint of
Sterling Publishers (P) Ltd.
L-10 Green Park Extension, New Delhi-110016
Tel : 6191023, 6191784/85; Fax : 91-11-6190028
E-mail: sterlin.gpvb@axcess.net.in
ghai@nde.vsnl.net.in

OSHO : The New Child
Compilation: Osho International Foundation
© Osho International Foundation, Zürich, 1991
First Edition 1998
ISBN 81 207 2086 5
Reprint 1999

Published by Sterling Publishers Pvt. Ltd., New Delhi-110016.
Printed at Prolific Incorporated, New Delhi-110020.
Cover design Arun Gupta

TABLE OF CONTENTS

PART I
ROBOTS ARE OBEDIENT –
REBELS ARE DANGEROUS

Conditioning: A Substitute for Intelligence

Beloved Osho,
Are idiots born or trained?

It is a complicated question. Almost ninety percent of idiots are trained. Ten percent are born. And the ten percent are born because of those ninety percent who have been trained.

Man from his very beginning has lived a very weird life – weird in the sense that somehow he needs idiots. If you don't have idiots you will not have the so-called wise men. If you don't have idiots, you will not have the giants of intellect. It becomes almost a necessity that the category of idiots should remain.

Nobody has looked into the deeper layers of how society has functioned up to now. But the way it has functioned can only be described as utterly criminal. Society needs categories, hierarchies. It has always been a competitive society, and the very idea of competition is dangerous to human beings. You call one man an idiot only in comparison -- in comparison to someone who seems to be intelligent.

A small boy told me – I was a guest in his house; I was sitting in the garden in the evening and he was the only child of the family. He was not more than six years old. I asked him, "What is your name?"

He said, "Up to now I used to think that my name was 'Don't!' Now I have started going to school, and there I discovered that it is not my name."

He is saying something tremendously important. Whatever a child is doing, the adults are there to say, "Don't do it!" Nobody is allowed to blossom according to his own intrinsic nature. And that is the fundamental cause of creating so many idiots in the world. But they do serve a certain purpose. If people were allowed to blossom according to their nature without any comparison and without any ideals and without enforced discipline, do you think anybody in the whole world would have accepted Adolf Hitler as a leader?

You need to look at your leaders. The idiots have been an absolute necessity for a few people to proclaim their egos, for a few people to rise high and become Nobel Prize winners. Just think for a moment – if everybody were living according to their own nature, not trying to be somebody else, a tremendous intelligence would explode within them. It is the fundamental law of life and existence.

It is good that flowers don't listen to your teachers and your leaders and your politicians. Otherwise they would say to the roses, "What are you doing? Become a lotus!" Roses are not so foolish. But if, just for argument's sake, roses did start trying to become lotuses, what would happen? Two things are certain: there would be no roses, because their whole energy would be involved in becoming lotuses, and the second thing, a rosebush cannot produce a lotus. It is not in the inbuilt program of its seed.

Have you ever come across a tree that you can say is an idiot? Or that it is very intelligent, a great giant, deserves a Nobel Prize? Man has been distracted. Everybody from your parents to your teachers, the school, the college, the university, your religion, your preachers, your neighbors – everybody is trying to make you somebody else, whom you cannot become. You can only become yourself, or you can miss becoming, be just an idiot.

I call this whole history of mankind a long, unjustified crime against every human individual. It has served the vested interests: the people who are in power, the people who are scholars, which is another kind of power, the people who are rich, which is another kind of power. They would not like everybody to be centered in himself because a man centered in himself cannot be exploited, cannot be enslaved, cannot be humiliated, cannot be forced to grow a canceric sense of guilt. These are the reasons humanity has not been allowed its growth.

From childhood, everybody is condemned – whatever he says, whatever he does, it is never right. Naturally he becomes afraid of saying anything, of doing anything on his own. He is appreciated if he is obedient, he is appreciated if he follows the rules and the regulations made by others. Everybody appreciates him. This is the strategy: condemn the man if he is trying to stand on his own feet and appreciate the man if he is just an imitator. Naturally his inner seed, his potentiality, will never have a chance to grow.

I am reminded of my own childhood. If I was sitting silently, somebody – and in India there are still big families, joint families; in my family there were at least fifty people – somebody was bound to come by and ask, "Why are you sitting silently?" Strange, I cannot sit silently, and if I make a noise and jump around the house... "Are you mad? Why are you jumping around the house?" Seeing the situation I decided that it would be better to begin the fight from the very beginning, because once you get caught with these people it will be very difficult to come out of the crowd.

My father was very much amazed. He said, "You never answer the question. On the contrary, you ask another question."

I said, "I have figured it out: when I am sitting silently and you ask, 'Why are you sitting silently?' I will not answer. I will ask, 'Why should I not sit silently? You have to answer. You are a grownup man, experienced – I am just a child. You answer me – why should I not sit silently?' " The whole family by and by understood... "You cannot get any statement from this boy. He immediately turns the question around and you are in trouble." They stopped asking me anything.

The situation came to the point that I might be sitting, and my mother would say, "I don't see anybody in the house" – and I was sitting in front of her! "I need vegetables; somebody should go and fetch vegetables."

I would say, "If I see anybody, I will tell you." I was taken as almost absent. And I proved it – because unless you prove it, it is very difficult. In the beginning they used to send me: "Go to the market. It is the season of beautiful mangoes. Bring mangoes."

I would go to the shop with the worst mangoes and ask, "Just give me the worst ones and charge me for the best ones."

Even those shopkeepers were amazed: "What kind of customer are you?"

I said, "What kind of customer? You have seen many customers... I am a unique customer."

And the man was perfectly happy to give me the rotten mangoes and charge the price for the best. I would come home and show those rotten mangoes and say, "These are the best, and I have paid for them." And they were stinking.

My mother would say, "Just throw them out!"

I said, "Why throw them out? There is a beggar woman, I can go and give them to her." Even the beggar woman would not accept them.

She would say, "Never come to me, because whenever you come you bring something rotten. Throw them to the dogs." And I was very much surprised that even dogs were afraid of me. If I threw something towards them, they would escape!

Slowly they settled that, "It is better to let him be, whatever he is. One thing is certain, he is going to be nobody special in life."

They were right. I have proved their prophecy.

I am nobody special in life.

But who cares about being special?

I am myself and that's enough, more than enough.

Each moment of my life I had to struggle to protect myself; if we don't do that everybody is ready to cut our roots. It is very difficult to find human beings in society who will allow you the freedom to be yourself. That has created a retardedness all over the world.

Nations need idiots; otherwise who is going to fight the wars? The world needs idiots; otherwise, how are people going to become richer and richer on the labor, on the blood of others? This civilization needs as many unintelligent people as possible; otherwise, who is going to be a Catholic, who is going to be a Protestant, who is going to be a Hindu, who is going to be a Mohammedan?

The whole structure of the society has been managed in such

a way that a very few people exploit millions of people. And they have given consolations to those who have been exploited: "It is because of your past life's evil acts." You don't know anything about your past life, so this is a good consolation: "What can I do?" Or they say, "This is a fire test of your faith in God. Be contented as you are and you will be rewarded a thousandfold beyond death." Religions have either taken refuge in the past... Jainism, Buddhism, Hinduism, they are all past-oriented. Or the other three religions – Christianity, Mohammedanism, Judaism – have taken refuge beyond death.

There is not much difference. All that is happening is happening in life and they are postponing it, either before birth or after death. The strategy is the same. The whole purpose is so that you allow people to exploit you, you allow people to drink your blood with the deep contentment that "this is how things are."

I want to say to you very emphatically that all these religions have played into the hands of the vested interests. All your priests are nothing but servants of your politicians. The whole history of mankind has been a disaster. And unless we start revolting as individuals, dropping all nationalities, all religions, all races, and declare that this whole globe belongs to us and all the lines of the map are bogus and false, unless individuals start changing the whole educational system...

The educational system should teach you the art of living, it should teach you the art of loving, it should teach you the art of meditation, it should teach you finally the art of dying gloriously. Your education system is not educational. It only creates clerks, stationmasters, postmen, soldiers, and you call it education. You have been deceived. But the deception has been going on so long that you have completely forgotten. And you are still going on in the same old rut.

I raise my hand against the whole past of mankind. It has not been civilized, it has not been human. It has not been in any way helpful for people to blossom, it has not been a spring. It has been a calamity, a crime committed on a vast scale...

But somebody has to stand against it, and somebody has to make the point: We disown our past. And we will start living according to our own inner being and create our own future. We will not allow the past to create our future.

Hymie Goldberg buys himself a fancy pair of Italian shoes in a Beverly Hills boutique, and wears them home to show them off to Becky.

Becky does not appear even to notice the new shoes, so Hymie waits until she is in bed and then walks in, stark naked except for the shoes.

Posing, he exclaims, "It is about time you paid some attention to what my prick is pointing at!"

Looking down at the shoes, Becky replies, "It is too bad you didn't buy a hat!"

In the middle of his sermon the priest stops, sniffs the air, and then holding his nose, calls the head usher to the front. "Please go through the church," says the priest, "and see if some stray dog stole in, stooled, and then stole out again."

The usher immediately begins his inspection and after some minutes comes back to make his report. "No, Father," he says, "I did not see where some stray dog stole in, stooled, and stole out again. But I did see some very positive signs where some creeping cat crept into the crypt, crapped, and crept out again."

I would like you to accept only one prayer, and that is laughter, because when you are laughing totally you are in the present. You cannot laugh in the future and you cannot laugh in the past. All those people who have created this retarded humanity have taken away all juice, all laughter, all smiles, and dragged everybody into being inauthentic. And if you are inauthentic, insincere, you can never grow the seed that has been given to you by this great compassionate universe.

An unshaven, dirty, bedraggled panhandler, with bloodshot eyes and teeth half gone, asks Paddy for a dime. "Do you drink, smoke, or gamble?" asks Paddy.

"Mister," says the bum, "I don't touch a drop, or smoke the filthy weed, or bother with evil gambling."

"Okay," says Paddy. "If you will come home with me I will give you a dollar."

As they enter the house, Maureen takes Paddy aside and hisses, "How dare you bring that terrible-looking specimen into our home!?"

"Darling," says Paddy, "I just wanted you to see what a man looks like who does not drink, does not smoke, and does not gamble."

Life should be not a serious thing. It should be a deep playfulness – fun. And every individual should be allowed absolute freedom to be himself. The only restriction will be that you cannot interfere in another individual's life sphere – it may be your wife, it may be your husband, it may be your child, it does not matter. A tremendous respect for the individual is to me the essential core of being truly religious. Be yourself and let others be themselves and this life, this planet, can become the lotus paradise herenow.

But something has to be done and done very soon, because all those idiots are preparing for a global suicide. Unless you revolt against the past, and the whole heritage of the past, you cannot save humanity, these beautiful trees, these birds singing, this small planet which has just developed to the stage of being conscious.

Scientists guess that there may be millions of other planets in the universe, but there is not even a single piece of evidence yet... The only evidence of life growing to this stage of consciousness – of love, of silence, of experiencing the cosmos – has happened on this small earth. At any cost, this earth and the people of this earth have to be saved from the calamity that is coming from your whole past. An absolute discontinuity is needed; all history books should be burnt.

The whole educational system should be centered on playfulness, on love, on freedom, on consciousness, and a tremendous respect for everything that is alive. This is my vision.

Time is very short. Those idiots have been working for thousands of years and they have come to a point where they are capable of destroying this earth seven times. So much destructive force is accumulating that unless a few individuals gather courage and revolt against all that is past... I am not telling you to choose, to choose that which is good and leave that which is bad. They are altogether; you cannot do that. The past has to be simply erased, as if we are on the earth for the first time and there has been no history. That is the only possibility of creating a beautiful world full of love, full of fragrance, with a deep respect for everybody. The past has lived centered on hate. The future can live only if it is centered on love. The past has been unconscious. The future can only be conscious.

To many this may seem an almost impossible dream. But remember, whatever you are is not because of the politicians, is not because of the priests. Whatever you are, if some flame is still alive in you, it is because of the poets, the dreamers, the mystics.

We can either die with the past or we can be reborn with a new future. Clean yourself and become Adam and Eve again. Disobey God again. Only then is there a possibility for this vision to become a reality.

Don't be concerned about the whole world. If we can create the idea of revolt in a small minority in the world, that will do. A single seed can make the whole earth green, and a single man in revolt can create a totally new world, a totally new humanity.

I am not in favor of any organized revolution because all organizations basically destroy the individual. I am in favor of the individual and his dignity. There is nobody above the individual. We have to take this tremendous quantum leap from organized living to individual flowering. It is possible. If it is possible for me – because I don't belong to any religion and I don't belong to any nation and I don't belong to any kind of organization – it is possible for you too. And if this fire of individuality spreads, it can become a wildfire, because deep down every individual is suffering. He wants to revolt against all that has been repressed, all that has been imposed on him.

And you will not find a better moment. This century is coming to its end, and one thing is certain, the old world cannot continue to live. All the prophets have been declaring the end of the world in the year 2000. None of them has said a single word about what happens beyond this century.

I want it to be clear to you, to my people around the earth, that the old world does not mean the planet. The old world means the old structure of humanity. It is going to die. But if we can save a few individuals, a new beginning is very close. Rather than being concerned with the old, rejoice for the new.

Om Mani Padme Hum, Session 10,
December 26, 1987

The Politics of Misery

Beloved Osho,
Does a child not have as much right to privacy and free-
dom from parental conditioning as the parents expect for
themselves?

It is one of the most fundamental problems facing humanity today.
The future depends on how we solve it. It has never been encountered
before. For the first time man has come of age, a certain maturity
has happened – and as you become mature you have to face new
problems.

Slowly, slowly, as man progressed, he became aware of many
kinds of slavery. Only recently in the West have we become aware
that the greatest slavery is that of the child. It was never thought
of before; it is not mentioned in any scripture of the world. Who
could have thought... a child and a slave? A slave to his own parents,
who love him, who sacrifice themselves for the child? It would have
looked ridiculous, utter nonsense! But now, as psychological insight
has deepened into the human mind and its functioning, it has become
absolutely clear that the child is the most exploited person; nobody
has been exploited more than the child. And of course he is being
exploited behind a façade of love.

And I don't say that the parents are aware that they are exploiting
the child, that they are imposing a slavery on the child, that they
are destroying the child, that they are making him stupid, unintelligent, that their whole effort of conditioning the child as a Hindu,
as a Mohammedan, as a Christian, as a Jaina, as a Buddhist, is
inhuman; they are not aware of it, but that does not make any
difference as far as the facts are concerned.

The child is being conditioned by the parents in ugly ways, and of course the child is helpless: he depends on the parents. He cannot rebel, he cannot escape, he cannot protect himself. He is absolutely vulnerable; hence he can be easily exploited.

Parental conditioning is the greatest slavery in the world. It has to be completely uprooted, only then will man be able for the first time to be really free, truly free, authentically free, because the child is the father of the man. If the child is brought up in a wrong way then the whole of humanity goes wrong. The child is the seed: if the seed itself is poisoned and corrupted by well-intentioned people, well-wishing people, then there is no hope for a free human individual, then that dream can never be fulfilled.

What you think you have is not individuality, it is only personality. It is something cultivated in you, in your nature, by your parents, the society, the priest, the politician, the educators. The educator, from the kindergarten to the university, is in the service of the vested interests, is in the service of the establishment. His whole purpose is to destroy every child in such a way, to cripple every child in such a way, that he adjusts to the established society.

There is a fear. The fear is that if the child is left unconditioned from the very beginning he will be so intelligent, he will be so alert, aware, that his whole life-style will be of rebellion. And nobody wants rebels; everybody wants obedient people.

Parents love the obedient child. And remember, the obedient child is almost always the most stupid child. The rebellious child is the intelligent one, but he is not respected or loved. The teachers don't love him, the society does not give him respect; he is condemned. Either he has to compromise with the society or he has to live in a kind of self-guilt. Naturally, he feels that he has not been good to his parents, he has not made them happy.

Remember perfectly well, the parents of Jesus were not happy with Jesus, the parents of Gautam the Buddha were not happy with Gautam the Buddha. These people were so intelligent, so rebellious, how could their parents be happy with them?

And each child is born with such great possibilities and potential that if he is allowed and helped to develop his individuality without any hindrance from others we will have a beautiful world, we will have many Buddhas and many Socrateses and many Jesuses, we will have a tremendous variety of geniuses. The genius happens very rarely not because the genius is rarely born, no; the genius rarely happens because it is very difficult to escape from the conditioning process of the society. Only once in a while does a child somehow manage to escape from its clutches.

Every child is being enveloped by the parents, by the society, by the teachers, by the priests, by all the vested interests – enveloped in many layers of conditioning. He is given a certain religious ideology: he is forced to become a Jew or a Christian or a Hindu or a Mohammedan. It is not his choice. And whenever somebody is forced with no choice of his own you are crippling the person, you are destroying his intelligence; you are not giving him a chance to choose, you are not allowing him to function intelligently; you are managing it in such a way that he will function only mechanically. He will be a Christian, but he is not Christian by choice. And what does it mean to be a Christian if it is not your choice?

The few people who followed Jesus, who went with him, were courageous people. They were the only Christians: they risked their lives, they went against the current, they lived dangerously; they were ready to die, but they were not ready to compromise.

The few people who went with Gautam Buddha were real Buddhists, but now there are millions of Christians around the world and millions of Buddhists around the world and they are all bogus, they are pseudo. They are bound to be pseudo – it is forced on them. They are enveloped in a certain religious ideology, then they are enveloped in a certain political ideology – they are told that they are Indians, that they are Iranians, that they are Chinese, that they are Germans – a certain nationality is imposed on them. And humanity is one, the earth is one.

But the politicians wouldn't like it to be one because if the earth is one then the politicians with all their politics have to disappear. Then where will all these presidents and prime ministers go? They can exist only if the world remains divided.

Religion is one, but then what will happen to the Polack Pope, to all the stupid shankaracharyas, to Ayatollah Khomeiniac? What will happen to all these people? They can exist only if there are many religions, many churches, many cults, many creeds.

There are three hundred religions on the earth and at least three thousand sects of these religions. Then of course there is a possibility for many priests, bishops, archbishops, high priests, shankaracharyas to exist. This possibility will disappear.

And I tell you, religiousness is one! It has nothing to do with any Bible, any Veda, any Gita. It has something to do with a loving heart, with an intelligent being. It has something to do with awareness, meditativeness. But then all the vested interests will suffer.

Hence parents who belong to a certain establishment, a certain nation, a certain church, a certain denomination, are bound to force their ideas on the children. And the strange thing is that the children are always more intelligent than the parents, because the parents belong to the past and the children belong to the future. The parents are already conditioned, enveloped, covered. Their mirrors are covered with so much dust that they don't reflect anything; they are blind.

Only a blind man can be a Hindu or a Mohammedan or a Jaina or a Christian. A man with eyes is simply religious. He does not go to the church or to the temple or to the mosque; he will not worship all kinds of stupid images. All kinds of gods, all kinds of superstitions! Parents carry all these. When a child is born he is a clean slate, a tabula rasa; nothing is written on him. That's his beauty: the mirror is without any dust. He can see more clearly.

Mum: 'Jimmy, did you fall over with your new trousers on?'

Jimmy: 'Yes, Mum, there wasn't time to take them off.'

The first-grade teacher was talking to her class about nature and she called it 'The World Around You'. She asked little Helen in the first row, 'Now, Helen tell everyone in the class. Are you animal, vegetable or mineral?'

'I'm not any of those,' she replied promptly. 'I'm a real live girl!'

A little fellow who was fishing off the end of a pier lost his balance while trying to land a fish and fell in the lake. Several men who were also fishing nearby rushed to his aid and pulled him out.

'How did you come to fall in?' one of the men asked him.
'I didn't come to fall in,' the kid said. 'I came to fish!'

A large family was finally able to move into a more spacious home.

Some time later an uncle asked his nephew, 'How do you like your new house?'

'Just fine,' replied the lad. 'My brother and I have our own rooms and so do my sisters. But poor Mom, she's still stuck in the same room with Dad!'

Every child is born intelligent, clear, clean, but we start heaping rubbish on him.

He has much more right than the parents because he is beginning his life. The parents are already burdened, they are already crippled, they are already depending on crutches. He has more right to be his own self. He needs privacy, but parents don't allow him any privacy; they are very afraid of the child's privacy. They are continuously poking their noses into the child's affairs; they want to have their say about everything.

The child needs privacy because all that is beautiful grows in privacy. Remember it: it is one of the most fundamental laws of life. The roots grow underground; if you take them out of the ground they start dying. They need privacy, absolute privacy. The child grows in the mother's womb in darkness, in privacy. If you bring the child into the light, among the public, he will die. He needs nine months of absolute privacy. Everything that needs growth needs privacy. A grown-up person does not need as much privacy because he is already grown-up, but a child needs much more privacy. But he is not left alone at all.

Parents are very worried whenever they see that the child is missing or is alone; they immediately become concerned. They are afraid, because if the child is alone he will start developing his individuality. He always has to be kept within limits so that the parents can go on watching, because their very watching does not allow his individuality to grow; their watching covers him, envelops him with a personality.

Personality is nothing but an envelope. It comes from a beautiful word, persona; persona means a mask. In Greek dramas the actors used masks. Sona means sound, per means through. They used to speak through the mask; you could not see their real faces, you could only hear their voices. Hence the mask was called a persona because the sound was heard through it, and out of persona comes the word 'personality'.

The child has to be continuously on guard because he is being watched. You can see it yourself: if you are taking a bath you are a totally different person – in your bathroom you can put aside your mask. Even grown-up people who are very serious start singing, humming. Even grown-up people start making faces in the mirror! You are in private – you are perfectly aware that you have locked the door – but if you suddenly become aware that somebody is watching through the keyhole, an immediate change will happen to you. You will again become serious, the song will disappear, you will not be making faces in the mirror; you will start behaving as you are supposed to behave. This is the personality – you are back in the envelope.

A child needs immense privacy, as much as possible, a maximum of privacy, so that he can develop his individuality uninterfered with. But we are trespassing on the child, continuously trespassing. The parents are continuously asking, 'What are you doing? What are you thinking?' Even thinking! They even have to look in your mind.

There are a few tribes in the Far East where each child has to tell his dreams every morning to the parents, because even in the dreams he cannot be left alone. He may be dreaming wrong dreams, he may be thinking things which he should not think; the parents have to be reported to.

The early morning ritual is that first thing before breakfast he has to relate his dreams – what he has seen in the night.

Psychoanalysis is a very late development in the West, but in the East, in these Far Eastern tribes, psychoanalysis has been practiced by the parents for thousands of years. And of course the poor child does not know the symbology so he simply relates the dream as it is. He does not know what it means; only the parents know. But this is going too far. It is encroaching upon him, it is inhuman; it is overlapping on somebody's space.

Just because the child is dependent on you for food, for clothes, for shelter, do you think you have the right to do it? – because if the child says that he has seen that he was flying in his dream, the parents immediately know that that is a sexual dream. Now they will curb his behavior more, they will discipline him more. They will give him an early-morning cold bath! They will teach him more about celibacy and they will teach him that 'If you are not celibate things will go wrong. If you think about sexuality you will lose all intelligence, you will go blind,' and all kinds of nonsense.

A child needs immense privacy. The parents should come only to help him, not to interfere. He should be allowed to do things or not to do things. Parents should only be alert that he does not do any harm to himself or to anybody else – that's enough. More than that is ugly.

A tourist drove into a small town and spoke to a boy who was sitting on a bench in front of the post office.

'How long have you lived here?' the tourist asked.

'About twelve years,' the boy replied.

'It sure is an out-of-the-way place, isn't it?' the tourist asked.

'It sure is,' the boy said.

'There isn't much going on,' the tourist said. 'I don't see anything here to keep you busy.'

'Neither do I,' the boy said. 'That's why I like it.'

The children like very much to be left alone; spaciousness is needed for their growth. Yes, parents have to be alert, cautious, so that no harm happens to the child, but this is a negative kind of cautiousness – they are not to interfere positively. They have to give the child a great longing to inquire about truth, but they have not to give him an ideology that gives him the idea of truth. They should not teach him about truth, they should teach him how to inquire about truth. Inquiry should be taught, investigation should be taught, adventure should be taught.

The children should be helped so that they can ask questions and the parents should not answer those questions unless they really know. And even if they know they should say it as Buddha used to say it to his disciples: 'Don't believe in what I say! This is my experience, but the moment I say it to you it becomes false because for you it is not an experience. Listen to me, but don't believe. Experiment, inquire, search. Unless you yourself know, your knowledge is of no use; it is dangerous. A knowledge which is borrowed is a hindrance.'

But that's what parents go on doing: they go on conditioning the child.

No conditioning is needed for the children, no direction has to be given to them. They have to be helped to be themselves, they have to be supported, nourished, strengthened. A real father, a real mother, real parents will be a blessing to the child. The child will feel helped by them so that he becomes more rooted in his nature, more grounded, more centered, so that he starts loving himself rather than feeling guilty about himself, so that he respects himself.

Remember, unless a person loves himself he cannot love anybody else in the world, unless a child respects himself he cannot respect anybody else. That's why all your love is bogus and all your respect is pseudo, phony. You don't respect yourself, how can you respect anybody else? Unless love for yourself is born within your being it will not radiate to others. First you have to become a light unto yourself, then your light will spread, will reach others.

It was examination day at school and a bad-tempered teacher was questioning a small boy about his knowledge of plants and flowers. The boy was unable to answer any question correctly. In frustration, the teacher turned to his assistant and shouted, 'Go and bring me a handful of hay!'

As the assistant turned to go out, the small boy cried, 'And for me, just a small coffee, please!'

A Polack was driving along a country road when his car broke down. While he was fixing it, a small boy approached and asked, 'What is that?'

'It's a jack,' said the Polack.

'My father has two of those,' said the boy.

Then a minute later he asked again, 'And what is that?'

'That's a torch.'

'Oh, my father has two of those too. And over there? Is that a spanner?'

'Yes,' said the man, irritably.

'My father has two of those.'

The conversation went on in this vein for some time. Finally the repair was finished and the Polack got up and went to piss at the side of the road. As he was pissing he pointed to his reproductive machinery and asked, 'Does your father have two of these too?'

'Of course not!' said the boy. 'But he has one that is twice as long!'

Children are immensely intelligent, they just need a chance! They need opportunities to grow, the right climate. Every child is born with the potential of enlightenment, with the potential of becoming awakened, but we destroy it.

This has been the greatest calamity in the whole history of man. No other slavery has been as bad as the slavery of the child and no other slavery has taken as much juice out of humanity as the slavery of the child, and this is also going to be the most difficult task for humanity: to get rid of it.

Unless we arrange the whole of society in a totally different way, unless a radical change happens and the family disappears and gives place to a commune, it will not be possible.

Once this old pattern of family disappears into a more multi-dimensional set-up, humanity can have a new birth. A new man is needed and the new man will bring the very paradise that in the past we were hoping for in some other life. Paradise can be herenow, but we have to bring about a new child.

Zen, Zest, Zip, Zap & Zing, Session 14
January 9, 1981

How Guilt is Built

Beloved Osho,
Why are parents so cruel to their children? Is there any
sense in making them responsible? And how can one avoid
making the same mistake?

Parents are cruel to their children because parents have some investment in them. Parents have some ambitions they would like to fulfill through their children – that's why they are cruel. They want to use the children. The moment you want to use somebody, you are bound to be cruel. In the very idea of using somebody as a means, cruelty has entered, violence has come in.

Never treat another person as a means, because each person is an end unto himself.

Parents are cruel because they have ideas: they want their children to be this and that. They would like their children to be rich, famous, respected; they would like their children to fulfill their unfulfilled egos. Their children are going to be their journeys.

The father wanted to be rich but could not succeed, and now death is approaching; sooner or later he will be cut off from life. He feels frustrated: he has not yet arrived. He was still searching and seeking... and now comes death – this looks so unjust. He would like his son to carry on the work, because his son represents him. He is his blood, he is his projection, his part – he is his immortality. Who knows about the soul? Nobody is definite about it. People believe, but belief is out of fear, and deep down the doubt remains.

Each belief carries the doubt in itself. Without the doubt there cannot be any belief. To repress the doubt, we create the belief –

but the doubt remains gnawing in the heart like a worm in the apple; it goes on eating inside you, it goes on rotting you from the inside. Who knows about God and who knows about soul? They may not be.

The only immortality known to man is through children – that is actual. The father knows, "I will be living in my son. I will be dead, soon I will be under the earth, but my son will be here. And my desires have remained unfulfilled." He imposes those desires, implants those desires in the consciousness of his son: "You have to fulfill them. If you fulfill them, I will be happy. If you fulfill them, you have paid your debts to your father. If you don't fulfill them, you have betrayed me."

This is from where cruelty comes in. Now, the father starts molding the child according to his desire. He forgets that the child has his own soul, that the child has his own individuality, that the child has his own inner growth to unfold. The father imposes his ideas. He starts destroying the child.

And he thinks he loves. He loves only his ambition. He loves the son also because he is going to become instrumental; he will be a means. This is what cruelty is.

You ask me: *Why are parents, so cruel to their children?*

They cannot help it, because they have ideas, ambitions, desires – unfulfilled. They want to fulfill them, they want to go on living through their children. Naturally, they prune, they cut, they mold, they give a pattern to the children. And the children are destroyed.

That destruction is bound to happen – unless a new human being arises on the earth, who loves for love's sake; unless a new parenthood is conceived: you love the child just for the sheer joy of it, you love the child as a gift from God. You love the child because God has been so... such a blessing to you. You love the child because the child is life, a guest from the unknown who has nestled into your house, into your being, who has chosen you as the nest. You are grateful and you love the child. If you really love the child, you will not give your ideas to the child.

Love never gives any ideas, never any ideology. Love gives freedom. You will not mold. If your child wants to become a musician, you will not try to distract him. And you know perfectly well that being a musician is not the right kind of job to be in, that he will be poor, that he will never become very rich, that he will never become a Henry Ford. Or the child wants to be a poet and you know he will remain a beggar. You know it, but you accept it because you respect the child.

Love is always respectful. Love is reverence.

You respect, because if this is God's desire to be fulfilled through the child, then let it be so. You don't interfere, you don't come in the way. You don't say, "This is not right. I know life more, I have lived life – you are just ignorant of life and its experiences. I know what money means. Poetry is not going to give you money. Become a politician, rather, or at least become an engineer or a doctor." And the child wants to become a woodcutter, or the child wants to become a cobbler, or the child simply wants to become a vagabond, and he wants to enjoy life... rest under trees, and on the sea beaches, and roam around the world.

You don't interfere if you love; you say, "Okay, with my blessings you go. You seek and search your truth. You be whatsoever you want to be. I will not stand in your way. And I will not disturb you by my experiences – because my experiences are my experiences. You are not me. You may have come through me, but you are not me – you are not a copy of me. You are not to be a copy of me. You are not to imitate me. I have lived my life – you live your life. I will not burden you with my unlived experiences. I will not burden you with my unfulfilled desires. I will keep you light. And I will help you. Whatsoever you want to be, be, with all my blessings and with all my help."

The children come through you, but they belong to God, they belong to totality. Don't possess them. Don't start thinking as if they belong to you. How can they belong to you?

Once this vision arises in you, then...then there will be no cruelty.

You ask: *Why are parents so cruel to their children? Is there any sense in making them responsible?*

No, I am not saying there is any sense in making parents responsible; because they have suffered because of their parents and so on and so forth. Understanding is needed. Finding scapegoats is of no help. You cannot simply say, "I am destroyed because my parents have destroyed me – what can I do?" I know parents are destructive, but if you become alert and aware you can get out of that pattern that they have created and woven around you.

You always remain capable of getting out of any trap that has been put around you. Your freedom may have been encaged, but the freedom is such, is so intrinsic, that it cannot be utterly destroyed. It always remains, and you can find it again. Maybe it is difficult, arduous, hard, an uphill task, but it is not impossible.

There is no point in just throwing the responsibility, because that makes you irresponsible. That's what Freudian psychoanalysis has been doing to people – that is its harm. You go to the psychoanalyst and he makes you feel perfectly good, and he says, "What can you do? Your parents were such – your mother was such, your father was such, your upbringing was wrong. That's why you are suffering from all these problems." You feel good – now you are no more responsible.

Christianity has made you feel responsible for two thousand years, has made you feel guilty, that you are the sinner. Now psychoanalysis goes to the other extreme: it simply says you are not the sinner, you are not to feel guilty – you are perfectly okay. You forget all about guilt and you forget all about sin. Others are responsible!

Christianity has done much harm by creating the idea of guilt – now psychoanalysis is doing harm from the other extreme, by creating the idea of irresponsibility.

You have to remember: the parents were doing something because they were taught to do those things – their parents had been teaching them. They were brought up by parents also; they had not come from heaven directly. So what is the point of throwing the responsibility backwards? It doesn't help; it will not help to solve any problem. It will help only to unburden you from guilt. That is good, the good part; the beneficial part of psychoanalysis is that it unburdens you from guilt. And the harmful part is that it leaves you there; it does not make you feel responsible.

To feel guilty is one thing: to feel responsible is another thing. I teach you responsibility. What do I mean by responsibility? You are not responsible to your parents, and you are not responsible to any God, and you are not responsible to any priest – you are responsible to your inner being. Responsibility is freedom! Responsibility is the idea that "I have to take the reins of my life in my own hands. Enough is enough! My parents have been doing harm – whatsoever they could do they have done: good and bad, they have done both. Now I have become a mature person. I should take everything in my own hands and start living the way it arises in me. I should devote all my energies to my life now." And immediately you will feel a great strength coming to you.

Guilt makes you feel weak: responsibility makes you feel strong. Responsibility gives you heart again, confidence, trust.

And remember, if you stand on your own feet, only then will you one day be able to walk without feet and fly without wings; otherwise not.

And you ask: *And how can one avoid making the same mistakes?*

Just try to understand those mistakes. If you see the point, why they are committed, you will not commit them. Seeing a truth is transforming. Truth liberates. Just see the point why your parents have destroyed you. Their wishes were good, but their awareness was not good; they were not aware people. They wanted you to be happy, certainly, they wished you all happiness. That's why they wanted you to become a rich man, a respected man; that's why they curbed your desires, cut your desires, molded you, patterned you, structured you, gave you a character, repressed many things, enforced many things. They did whatsoever they could. Their wish was right: they wanted you to be happy, although they were not aware of what they were doing, although they themselves had never known what happiness is. They were unhappy people and unaware.

Their wish was good – don't feel angry about them. They did whatsoever they could. Feel sorry for them, but never angry at them.

Don't feel any rage! They were helpless! They were caught in a certain trap. They had not known what happiness is, but they had some idea that a happy person is one who has much money. They worked for it their whole lives; they wasted their whole lives in earning money, but they remained with that stupid idea that money brings happiness. And they tried to poison your being too. They were not thinking to poison you – they were thinking they were pouring elixir in you. Their dreams were good, their wishes were good, but they were unhappy people and unaware people – that's why they have done harm to you.

Now be aware. Search for happiness. Find out how to be happy. Meditate, pray, love. Live passionately and intensely! If you have known happiness, you will not be cruel to anybody – you cannot be. If you have tasted anything of life, you will never be destructive to anybody. How can you be destructive to your own children? You cannot be destructive to anybody at all.

If you have known awareness, then that's enough. You need not ask, "And how can one avoid making the same mistakes?" If you are not happy and aware, you cannot avoid making the same mistakes – you will make the same mistakes! You are bound to, you are doomed to make the same mistakes.

So I cannot give you a clue as to how to avoid – I can only give you an insight. The insight is: your parents were unhappy – please, you be happy. Your parents were unaware – you be aware. And those two things – awareness and happiness – are not really two things but two aspects of the same coin.

Start by being aware and you will be happy! And a happy person is a non-violent person.

And always remember: children are not adult; you should not expect adult things from children. They are children! They have a totally different vision, a different perspective. You should not start forcing your adultish attitudes upon them. Allow them to remain children, because they never will be again; and once lost, everybody feels nostalgia for the childhood, everybody feels those days were days of paradise. Don't disturb them. Sometimes it is difficult for you to accept the children's vision – because you have lost it yourself! A child is trying to climb a tree; what will you do? You immediately become afraid – he may fall, he may break his leg, or something may go wrong. And out of your fear you rush and you stop the child.

If you had known what joy it is to climb a tree, you would have helped so that the child could learn how to climb trees! You would have taken him to a school where it is taught how to climb trees. You would not have stopped him. Your fear is good – it shows love, that the child may fall, but to stop the child from climbing the tree is to stop the child from growing.

There is something essential about climbing trees. If a child has never been doing it, he will remain in some way poor, he will miss some richness – for his whole life. You have deprived him of something beautiful, and there is no other way to know about it! Later on it will become more difficult for him to climb in the tree: it will look stupid or foolish or ridiculous.

Let him climb the tree. And if you are afraid, help him, go and teach him. You also climb with him! Help him learn so he doesn't fall. And once in a while, falling from a tree is not so bad either. Rather than being deprived forever...

The child wants to go out in the rain and wants to run around the streets in the rain, and you are afraid he may catch a cold or get pneumonia or something – and your fear is right! So do something so that he is more resistant to colds. Take him to the doctor; ask the doctor what vitamins should be given to him so that he can run in the rains and enjoy and dance and there is no fear that he will catch cold or will get pneumonia. But don't stop him. To dance in the streets when it is raining is such a joy! To miss it is to miss something very valuable.

If you know happiness and if you are aware, you will be able to feel for the child, how he feels.

A child is jumping and dancing and shouting and shrieking, and you are reading your newspaper, your stupid newspaper. And you know what is there – it is always the same. But you feel disturbed. There is nothing in your newspaper, but you feel disturbed. You stop the child: "Don't shout! Don't disturb Daddy!" Daddy is doing something great – reading the newspaper! And you stop that running energy, that flow – you stop that glow, you stop life. You are being violent.

And I am not saying that the child has always to be allowed to disturb you. But out of a hundred times, ninety times you are unnecessarily disturbed. And if you don't disturb him those ninety times, the child will understand. When you understand the child, the child understands you – children are very, very responsive. When the child sees that he is never prevented, then once you say, "I am doing something please..." the child will know that it is not from a parent who is constantly looking to shout at him. It is from a parent who allows everything.

Children have a different vision.

"Now, I want it quiet," said the teacher, "so quiet you can hear a pin drop."

A deep silence descended on the classroom. After about two minutes an anguished voice from the back shouted, "For Pete's sake, let it drop!"

It was the little boy's first day at school, and as soon as his mother had left him, he burst into tears. Despite all efforts on the part of his teacher and the headmistress, he went on crying and crying until finally, just before lunch, the teacher said in exasperation, "For heaven's sake, shut up child! It's lunch time now, and then in a couple more hours you'll be going home and you'll see your mummy again."

At once the little boy stopped crying, "Will I?" he said. "I thought I had to stay here until I was sixteen!"

They have their vision, their understanding, their ways. Try to understand them. An understanding mind will always find a deep harmony arising between him and the child. It is the stupid, the unconscious, the non-understanding people, who go on remaining closed in their ideas and never look at the other's vision.

Children bring freshness into the world.

Children are new editions of consciousness.

Children are fresh entries of divinity into life. Be respectful, be understanding. And if you are happy and alert, there is no need to be worried about how not to commit the same mistakes – you will not commit them. But then you have to be totally different from your parents. Consciousness will bring that difference.

Walk Without Feet, Fly Without Wings & Think Without Mind, Session 2
January 2, 1978

PART II
CHILDREN – NEW EDITIONS OF CONSCIOUSNESS

Smack Your Own Bottom!

Beloved Osho,
How can the birth of a child be made as gentle as
possible?

When the child comes out of the womb, it is the greatest shock
of his life. Even death will not be this big a shock, because death
will come without warning. Death will come most probably when
he is unconscious. But while he is coming out of the mother's womb,
he is conscious. His nine months' long sleep, peaceful sleep, is
disturbed – and then you cut the thread which joins him with the
mother.

The moment you cut that thread that joins him with the mother,
you have created a fearful individual.

This is not the right way; but this is how it has been done up
to now. Unknowingly, this has helped the priest and the so-called
religions to exploit man.

The child should be taken away from the mother more slowly,
more gradually. There should not be that shock – and it can be
arranged. A scientific arrangement is possible.

There should not be glaring lights in the room, because the child
has lived for nine months in absolute darkness, and he has very
fragile eyes which have never seen light. And in all your hospitals
there are glaring lights, tube lights, and the child suddenly faces
the light... Most people are suffering from weak eyes because of
this; later on they have to use glasses. No animal needs them. Have
you seen animals with glasses reading the newspaper? Their eyes
are perfectly healthy their whole life, to the point of death. It is

only man... And the beginning is at the very beginning. No, the child should be given birth to in darkness, or in a very soft light, candles perhaps.

Darkness would be the best, but if a little light is needed, then candles will do.

And what have the doctors been doing up to now? They don't even give a little time for the child to be acquainted with the new reality. The way they welcome the child is so ugly. They hang the child with his feet in their hands and they slap his bottom. The idea behind this stupid ritual is that this will help the child to breathe – because in the mother's womb he was not breathing on his own; the mother was breathing for him, eating for him, doing everything for him.

To be welcomed into the world hanging upside down, with a slap on your bottom, is not a very good beginning.

But the doctor is in a hurry. Otherwise the child would start breathing on his own; he has to be left on the mother's belly, on top of the mother's belly. Before the joining thread is cut, he should be left on the mother's belly. He was inside the belly, beneath; now he is outside. That is not a great change. The mother is there, he can touch her, he can feel her. He knows the vibe. He is perfectly aware that this is his home. He has come out, but this is his home. Let him be with the mother a little longer, so he becomes acquainted with the mother from the outside; from the inside he knows her.

And don't cut the thread that joins him till he starts breathing on his own.

Right now, what is done? We cut the thread and slap the child so he has to breathe. But this is forcing him, this is violent, and absolutely unscientific and unnatural.

Let him first breathe on his own. It will take a few minutes. Don't be in such a hurry. It is a question of a man's whole life. You can smoke your cigarette two or three minutes later, you can whisper sweet nothings to your girlfriend a few minutes later. It is not going to harm anybody. What is the rush? You can't give him three minutes? A child needs no more than that. Just left on his own, within three minutes he starts breathing. When he starts breathing, he becomes confident that he can live on his own. Then you can cut the thread, it is useless now; it will not give a shock to the child.

Then the most significant thing is, don't put him in blankets and in a bed. No, for nine months he was without blankets, naked, without pillows, without bed sheets, without a bed – don't make such a change so quickly. He needs a small tub with the same solution of water that was in his mother's womb – it is exactly ocean water: the same amount of salt, the same amount of chemicals, exactly the same.

That is again a proof that life must have happened first in the ocean. It still happens in the oceanic water.

That's why when a woman is pregnant she starts eating salty things, because the womb goes on absorbing the salt – the child needs exactly the same salty water that exists in the ocean. So just make up the same water in a small tub, and let the child lie down in the tub, and he will feel perfectly welcomed. This is the situation he is acquainted with.

In Japan, one Zen monk has tried a tremendous experiment: helping a three-month-old child to swim. Slowly he has been coming down. First he tried with nine-month-old children, then with six-month-old children, now with three-month-old children. And I say to him that you are still far away. Even the child just born is capable of swimming, because he has been swimming in his mother's womb.

So give the child a chance, similar to the mother's womb. And he will be more confident; and no priest can exploit him so easily, telling him about hellfire, and all that nonsense.

The Rajneesh Bible, Volume I, Session 25
November 23, 1984

The Face of God

Beloved Osho,
How can one ensure that our children maintain their
original face?

The original face of every child is the face of God. Of course my God is not a Christian, a Hindu, a Jew. My God is not even a person but only a presence. It is less like a flower and more like fragrance. You can feel it but you cannot catch hold of it. You can be overwhelmed by it but you cannot possess it.

My God is not something objective, there.

My God is your very subjectivity, here.

My God can never be indicated by the word "that." He can only be indicated by the word "this." The God of my vision and experience is not to be searched for in the synagogues, temples, mosques, churches, in the Himalayas, in the monasteries. He is not there because He is always here. And you go on looking for Him there.

When I say every child's original face is the face of God, I am saying that God is synonymous with life, existence. Whatsoever is, is divine, sacred. And there is nothing else than God.

God is not to be understood as quantity, but as quality. You cannot measure it. You cannot make a statue of it, you cannot draw a picture of it. In that sense it is absolutely impersonal. And if you look at the faces of children when they arrive, fresh from the very source of life, you will see a certain presence which cannot be named – unnameable, indefinable.

The child is alive. You cannot define its aliveness, but it is there, you can feel it. It is so much there that howsoever blind you are you cannot miss it. It is fresh. You can smell the freshness around

39

a child. That fragrance slowly, slowly disappears. And if unfortunately the child becomes successful, a celebrity – a president, a prime minister, a pope – then the same child stinks.

He had come with a tremendous fragrance, immeasurable, indefinable, unnameable. You look into the eyes of a child – you cannot find anything deeper. The eyes of a child are an abyss, there is no bottom to them.

Unfortunately, the way society will destroy him, soon his eyes will be only superficial; because of layers and layers of conditioning, that depth, that immense depth will have disappeared long before. And that was his original face.

The child has no thoughts. About what can he think? Thinking needs a past, thinking needs problems. He has no past, he has only future.

He has no problems yet, he is without problems. There is no possibility of thinking for him. What can he think?

The child is conscious but without thoughts.

This is the original face of the child.

Once this was your face too, and although you have forgotten it, it is still there within you, waiting someday to be rediscovered. I am saying rediscovered because you have discovered it many times in your previous lives, and again and again you go on forgetting it.

Perhaps even in this life there have been moments when you have come very close to knowing it, to feeling it, to being it. But the world is too much with us. Its pull is great – and there are a thousand and one directions the world is pulling you. It is pulling you in so many directions that you are falling apart. It is a miracle how people go on managing to keep themselves together. Otherwise their one hand will be going to the north, another hand to the south, their head must be going towards heaven; all their parts will be flying all over the place.

It is certainly a miracle how you go on keeping yourself together.

Perhaps the pressure from all sides is too much so that your hands and legs and heads cannot fly. You are pressed from everywhere.

Even if by chance you happen to meet your original face, you will not be able to recognize it, it will be such a stranger. Perhaps you come across it once in a while, just by accident, but you don't even say Hi! It is a stranger and perhaps deep down, a certain fear – that is always there with every stranger.

You are asking me how we can save the original face of our children.

You don't have to do anything directly.

Anything done directly will be a disturbance.

You have to learn the art of non-doing. That is a very difficult art. It is not something that you have to do to protect, to save, the original face of the child. Whatever you do will distort the original face. You have to learn non-doing; you have to learn to keep away, out of the way of the child. You have to be very courageous because it is risky to leave the child to himself.

For thousands of years we have been told, if the child is left to himself he will be a savage.

That is sheer nonsense. I am sitting before you – do you think I am a savage? And I have lived without being interfered with by my parents. Yes, there was much trouble for them and there will be much trouble for you too, but it is worth it.

The original face of the child is so valuable that any trouble is worth it. It is so priceless that whatsoever you have to pay for it, it is still cheap; you are getting it for nothing. And the joy on the day you find your child with his original face intact, with the same beauty that he had brought into the world, the same innocence, the same clarity, the same joyfulness, cheerfulness, the same aliveness... What more can you expect?

You cannot give anything to the child, you can only take. If you really want to give a gift to the child, this is the only gift possible: don't interfere. Take the risk and let the child go into the unknown, into the uncharted. It is difficult. Great fear grips the parents – who knows what will happen to the child?

Out of this fear they start molding a certain pattern of life for the child. Out of fear they start directing him into a particular way, towards a particular goal, but they don't know that because of their fear they are killing the child. He will never be blissful. And he will never be grateful to you; he will always carry a grudge against you.

Sigmund Freud has a great insight in this matter: he says, "Every culture respects the father. No culture on earth exists, or has ever existed, which has not propounded, propagated the idea that the father has to be respected." Sigmund Freud says, "This respect for the father arises because sometime back in prehistoric times the father must have been killed by the children just to save themselves from being crippled."

It is a strange idea, but very significant. He is saying that the respect is being paid to the father out of guilt, and that guilt has been carried for thousands of years. Somewhere... it is not a historical fact, but a meaningful myth, that young people must have killed their father and then repented – naturally, because he was their father; but he was driving them into ways where they were not happy.

They killed him, but then they repented. Then they started worshipping the spirits of the ancestors, fathers, forefathers, out of fear, because the ghosts of those can take revenge. And then slowly, slowly, it became a convention to be respectful towards the elders. But why?

I would like you to be respectful to the children.

The children deserve all the respect you can manage, because they are so fresh, so innocent, so close to godliness. It is time to pay respect to them, not to force them to pay respect to all kinds of corrupted people – cunning, crooked, full of shit – just because they are old.

I would like to reverse the whole thing: respect towards the children because they are closer to the source; you are far away. They are still original, you are already a carbon copy. And do you understand what it can do if you are respectful to children? Then through love and respect you can save them from going in any wrong direction – not out of fear but out of your respect and love.

My grandfather... I could not speak a lie to my grandfather because he respected me so much. When the whole family was against me I could at least depend on the old man. He would not bother about all the proofs that were against me. He would say, "I don't care what he has done. If he has done it, it must be right. I know him, he cannot do wrong."

And when he was with me of course the whole family had to shrink back. I would tell him the whole thing, and he would say, "There is no need to be worried. Do whatsoever you feel is right, because who else can decide? In your situation, in your place, only you can decide. Do whatsoever you feel is right, and always remember that I am here to support you, because I not only love you, I respect you too."

His respect towards me was the greatest treasure I could have received. When he was dying I was eighty miles away. He informed me that I should come immediately because there was not much time. I came quickly; within two hours I was there.

It was as if he was just waiting for me. He opened his eyes and he said, "I was just trying to continue to breathe so that you could reach me. Just one thing I want to say: I will not be here now to support you, and you will need support. But remember, wherever I am, my love and my respect will remain with you. Don't be afraid of anybody, don't be afraid of the world."

Those were his last words: "Don't be afraid of the world."

Respect the children, make them fearless.

But if you are yourself full of fear, how can you make them fearless? Don't force respect on them towards you because you are their father, you are their daddy, their mom, this and that.

Change this attitude and see what transformation respect can bring to your children. They will listen to you more carefully if you respect them. They will try to understand you and your mind more carefully if you respect them. They have to. And in no way are you imposing anything; so if by understanding they feel you are right and they follow you, they will not lose their original face.

The original face is not lost by going on a certain way. It is lost by children being forced, forced against their will.

Love and respect can sweetly help them to be more understanding about the world, can help them to be more alert, aware, careful – because life is precious, and it is a gift from existence. We should not waste it.

At the moment of death we should be able to say that we are leaving the world better, more beautiful, more graceful. But this is possible only if we leave this world with our original face, the same face with which we came into it.

From Darkness to Light, Session 6
March 5, 1985

The Budding of a Buddha

Beloved Osho,
How did You manage to stay with Your own clarity as a
child and not let Yourself become intimidated by the
grown-ups around You? Where did You get that courage
from?

Innocence is courage and clarity both.

There is no need to have courage if you are innocent. There is no need, either, for any clarity because nothing can be more clear, crystal clear, than innocence. So the whole question is how to protect one's own innocence.

Innocence is not something to be achieved. It is not something to be learned. It is not something like a talent: painting, music, poetry, sculpture. It is not like those things. It is more like breathing, something you are born with.

Innocence is everybody's nature. Nobody is born other than innocent. How can one be born other than innocent?

Birth means you have entered the world as a tabula rasa, nothing is written on you. You have only future, no past. That is the meaning of innocence. So first try to understand all the meanings of innocence.

The first is: no past, only future. You come with an innocent watcher into the world. Everybody comes in the same way, with the same quality of consciousness.

The question is, how did I manage so that nobody could corrupt my innocence, clarity; from where did I get this courage? How could I manage not to be humiliated by grown-ups and their world?

I have not done anything, so there is no question of how. It simply happened, so I cannot take the credit for it.

Perhaps it happens to everybody but you become interested in other things. You start bargaining with the grown-up world. They have many things to give to you; you have only one thing to give, and that is your integrity, your self-respect. You don't have much, a single thing – you can call it anything: innocence, intelligence, authenticity. You have only one thing.

And the child is naturally very much interested in everything he sees around. He is continuously wanting to have this, to have that; that is part of human nature. If you look at the small child, even a just-born baby, you can see he has started groping for something; his hands are trying to find out something. He has started the journey.

In the journey he will lose himself, because you can't get anything in this world without paying for it. And the poor child cannot understand that what he is giving is so valuable that if the whole world is on one side, and his integrity is on the other side, then too his integrity will be more weighty, more valuable. The child has no way to know about it. This is the problem, because what he has got he has simply got. He takes it for granted.

You are asking me how I managed not to lose my innocence and clarity. I have not done anything; just simply, from the very beginning.... I was a lonely child because I was brought up by my maternal grandfather and grandmother; I was not with my father and mother. Those two old people were alone and they wanted a child who would be the joy of their last days. So my father and mother agreed: I was their eldest child, the first-born; they sent me.

I don't remember any relationship with my father's family in the early years of my childhood. With these two old men – my grandfather and his old servant, who was really a beautiful man – and my old grandmother... these three people. And the gap was so big... I was absolutely alone. It was not company, it could not be company. They tried their hardest to be as friendly to me as possible but it was just not possible.

I was left to myself. I could not say things to them. I had nobody else, because in that small village my family were the richest; and it was such a small village – not more than two hundred people in all – and so poor that my grandparents would not allow me to mix with the village children. They were dirty, and of course they were almost beggars. So there was no way to have friends. That caused a great impact. In my whole life I have never been a friend, I have never known anybody to be a friend. Yes, acquaintances I had.

In those first, early years I was so lonely that I started enjoying it; and it is really a joy. So it was not a curse to me, it proved a blessing. I started enjoying it, and I started feeling self-sufficient; I was not dependent on anybody.

I have never been interested in games for the simple reason that from my very childhood there was no way to play, there was nobody to play with. I can still see myself in those earliest years, just sitting.

We had a beautiful spot where our house was, just in front of a lake. Far away for miles, the lake... and it was so beautiful and so silent. Only once in a while would you see a line of white cranes flying, or making love calls, and the peace would be disturbed; otherwise, it was exactly the right place for meditation. And when they would disturb the peace – a love call from a bird... after his call the peace would deepen, it would become deeper.

The lake was full of lotus flowers, and I would sit for hours so self-content, as if the world did not matter: the lotuses, the white cranes, the silence...

And my grandparents were very aware of one thing, that I enjoyed my aloneness. They had continuously been seeing that I had no desire to go to the village to meet anybody, or to talk with anybody. Even if they wanted to talk, my answers were yes or no; I was not interested in talking either. So they became aware of one thing, that I enjoyed my aloneness, and it was their sacred duty not to disturb me.

It happens with children that you tell them, "Be silent because your father is thinking, your grandfather is resting. Be quiet, sit silently." In my childhood it happened the opposite way. Now I cannot answer why and how; it simply happened. That's why I said it simply happened – the credit does not go to me.

All those three old people were continuously making signs to each other: "Don't disturb him – he is enjoying so much." And they started loving my silence.

Silence has its vibe; it is infectious, particularly a child's silence which is not forced, which is not because you are saying, "I will beat you if you create any nuisance or noise." No, that is not silence. That will not create the joyous vibration that I am talking about, when a child is silent on his own, enjoying for no reason, his happiness is uncaused; that creates great ripples all around.

In a better world, every family will learn from children. You are in such a hurry to teach them. Nobody seems to learn from them, and they have much to teach you. And you have nothing to teach them.

Just because you are older and powerful you start making them just like you without ever thinking about what you are, where you have reached, what your status is in the inner world. You are a pauper; and you want the same for your child also?

But nobody thinks; otherwise people would learn from small children. Children bring so much from the other world because they are such fresh arrivals. They still carry the silence of the womb, the silence of the very existence.

So it was just a coincidence that for seven years I remained undisturbed – no one to nag me, to prepare me for the world of business, politics, diplomacy. My grandparents were more interested in leaving me as natural as possible – particularly my grandmother. She is one of the causes – these small things affect all your life patterns – she is one of the causes of my respect for the whole of womanhood.

She was a simple woman, uneducated, but immensely sensitive. She made it clear to my grandfather and the servant: "We all have lived a certain kind of life which has not led us anywhere. We are as empty as ever, and now death is coming close." She insisted, "Let this child be uninfluenced by us. What influence can we...? We can only make him like us, and we are nothing. Give him an opportunity to be himself."

I am tremendously grateful to that old woman. My grandfather was again and again worried that sooner or later he was going to be responsible: "They will say, 'We left our child with you and you have not taught him anything.'"

My grandmother did not even allow... because there was one man in the village who could at least teach me the beginnings of language, mathematics, a little geography. He was educated to the fourth grade – the lowest four of what was called primary education in India. But he was the most educated man in the town.

My grandfather tried hard: "He can come and he can teach him. At least he will know the alphabet, some mathematics, so when he goes to his parents they will not say that we just wasted seven years completely."

But my grandmother said, "Let them do whatsoever they want to do after seven years. For seven years he has to be just his natural self, and we are not going to interfere." And her argument was always, "You know the alphabet, so what? You know mathematics, so what? You have earned a little money; do you want him also to earn a little money and live just like you?"

That was enough to keep that old man silent. What to do? He was in a difficulty because he could not argue, and he knew that he would be held responsible, not she, because my father would ask him, "What have you done?" And actually that would have been the case, but fortunately he died before my father could ask.

But my father continuously was saying, "That old man is responsible, he has spoiled the child." But now I was strong enough, and I made it clear to him: "Before me, never say a single word against my maternal grandfather. He has saved me from being spoiled by you – that is your real anger. But you have other children – spoil them. And at the final stage you will say who is spoiled."

He had other children, and more and more children went on coming. I used to tease him, "You please bring one child more, make it a dozen."

Eleven children? People ask, "How many children?" Eleven does not look right; one dozen is more impressive." And in later years I used to tell him, "You go on spoiling all your children; I am wild, and I will remain wild."

What you see as innocence is nothing but wildness. What you see as clarity is nothing but wildness. Somehow I remained out of the grip of civilization.

And once I was strong enough... And that's why people insist, "Take hold of the child as quickly as possible, don't waste time because the earlier you take hold of the child, the easier it is. Once the child becomes strong enough, then to bend him according to your desires will be difficult."

And life has seven-year circles. By the seventh year the child is perfectly strong; now you cannot do anything. Now he knows where to go, what to do. He is capable of arguing. He is capable of seeing what is right and what is wrong. And his clarity will be at the climax when he is seven. If you don't disturb his earlier years, then at the seventh he is so crystal clear about everything that his whole life will be lived without any repentance.

I have lived without any repentance. I have tried to find: Have I done anything wrong, ever? Not that people have been thinking that all that I have done is right, that is not the point: I have never thought anything that I have done was wrong. The whole world may think it was wrong, but to me there is absolute certainty that it was right; it was the right thing to do.

So there is no question of repenting the past. And when you don't have to repent the past you are free from it. The past keeps you entangled like an octopus because you go on feeling, "That thing I should not have done," or, "That thing which I was supposed to do and did not do..." All those things go on pulling you backwards.

I don't see anything behind me, no past.

If I say something about my past, it is simply factual memory, it has no psychological involvement. I am telling you as if I am telling you about somebody else. It is just factual; it has nothing to do with my personal involvement. It might have occurred to somebody else, it might have happened to somebody else.

So remember, a factual memory is not enslaving: psychological memory is. And psychological memory is made up of things that you think, or you have been conditioned to think, were wrong and you did them. Then there is a wound, a psychological wound.

From Darkness to Light, Session 2
March 1, 1985

50

Seven-year Free-wheeling Cycles

Beloved Osho,
What is the right way to help the child grow?

You will have to understand some significant growth patterns. Life
has seven-year cycles: it moves in seven-year circles just as the earth
makes one rotation on its axis in twenty-four hours. Now nobody
knows why not twenty-five, why not twenty-three. There is no way
to answer it; it is simply a fact.

The earth takes three hundred and sixty-five days to make one
round of the sun. Why three hundred and sixty-five? Nobody knows,
nobody needs to know. And it does not make any difference. If
it were taking four hundred days, what difference would it have
made to you?... or three hundred days...? The question would have
remained the same: Why?

So remember one thing: any question is absurd if with every answer
the question still remains the same. In twenty-four hours the earth
makes one turn on its own axis. Why? Make it twenty-five, make
it twenty-six, make it thirty, sixty – as much as you want – the
question till stands the same: why? Hence I call the question absurd;
it will always remain the same.

So don't ask me why life moves in seven-year circles. I don't
know. This much I know, that it moves in seven-year circles. And
if you understand those seven-year circles, you will understand a
great deal about human growth.

The first seven years are the most important because the foundation
of life is being laid. That's why all the religions are very much
concerned about grabbing children as quickly as possible.

The Jews will circumcise the child. What nonsense! But they are stamping the child as a Jew; that is a primitive way of stamping. You still do it on the cattle around here; I have seen stamps. Every owner stamps the cattle, otherwise they can get mixed up. It is a cruel thing. Red-hot steel has to be used to stamp the cattle's leather skin; it burns the skin. But then it becomes your possession; it cannot be lost, it cannot be stolen.

What is circumcision? It is stamping cattle. But these cattle are Jews.

Hindus have their own ways. All religions have their own ways. But it should be known whose cattle you are, who your shepherd is – Jesus? Moses? Mohammed? You are not your own master.

Those first seven years are the years when you are conditioned, stuffed with all kinds of ideas which will go on haunting you your whole life, which will go on distracting you from your potentiality, which will corrupt you, which will never allow you to see clearly. They will always come like clouds before your eyes, they will make everything confused.

Things are clear, very clear – existence is absolutely clear – but your eyes have layers upon layers of dust.

And all that dust has been arranged in the first seven years of your life when you were so innocent, so trusting, that whatsoever was told to you, you accepted as truth. And whatsoever has gone into your foundation will be very difficult for you to find later on: it has become almost part of your blood, bones, your very marrow. You will ask a thousand other questions but you will never ask about the basic foundations of your belief.

The first expression of love towards the child is to leave his first seven years absolutely innocent, unconditioned, to leave him for seven years completely wild, a pagan.

He should not be converted to Hinduism, to Mohammedanism, to Christianity. Anybody who is trying to convert the child is not compassionate, he is cruel: he is contaminating the very soul of a new, fresh arrival. Before the child has even asked questions he has been answered with ready-made philosophies, dogmas, ideologies.

This is a very strange situation. The child has not asked about God, and you go on teaching him about God. Why so much impatience? Wait!

If the child someday shows interest in God and starts asking about God, then try to tell him not only your idea of God – because nobody has any monopoly: put before him all the ideas of God that have been presented to different people by different ages, by different religions, cultures, civilizations.

Put before him all the ideas about God, and tell him, "You can choose between these, whichever appeals to you. Or you can invent your own, if nothing suits. If everything seems to have a flaw, and you think you can have a better idea, then invent your own. Or if you find that there is no way to invent an idea without loopholes, then drop the whole thing; there is no need. A man can live without God; there is no intrinsic necessity.

"Millions of people have lived without God. God is nothing that is inevitably needed by you. Yes, I have my idea; that too is in the combination of all these ideals in this collection. You can choose that, but I am not saying that my idea is the right idea. It appeals to me; it may not appeal to you."

There is no inner necessity that the son should agree with the father. In fact it seems far better that he should not agree. That's how evolution happens. If every child agrees with the father then there will be no evolution, because the father will agree with his own father, so everybody will be where God left Adam and Eve – naked, outside the gate of the garden of Eden. Everybody will be there.

Because sons have disagreed with their fathers, forefathers, with their whole tradition, man has evolved.

This whole evolution is a tremendous disagreement with the past.

The more intelligent you are, the more you are going to disagree.

But parents appreciate the child who agrees; they condemn the child who disagrees.

Up to seven years, if a child can be left innocent, uncorrupted by the ideas of others, then to distract him from his potential growth becomes impossible. The child's first seven years are the most vulnerable. And they are in the hands of parents, teachers, priests...

How to save children from parents, priests, teachers is a question of such enormous proportions that it seems almost impossible to find out how to do it.

It is not a question of helping the child.

It is a question of protecting the child.

If you have a child, protect the child from yourself. Protect the child from others who can influence him: at least up to seven years, protect him.

The child is just like a small plant, weak, soft: just a strong wind can destroy it, any animal can eat it up. You put a protective wiring around it, but that is not imprisoning, you are simply protecting. When the plant is bigger, the wires will be removed.

Protect the child from every kind of influence so that he can remain himself – and it is only a question of seven years, because then the first circle will be complete. By seven years he will be well-grounded, centered, strong enough.

You don't know how strong a seven-year-old child can be because you have not seen uncorrupted children, you have seen only corrupted children. They carry the fears, the cowardliness, of their fathers, mothers, their families. They are not their own selves.   If a child remains uncorrupted for seven years... You will be surprised to meet such a child. He will be as sharp as a sword. His eyes will be clear, his insight will be clear. And you will see a tremendous strength in him which you cannot find even in a seventy-year-old adult, because the foundations are shaky. In fact as the building goes on becoming higher and higher, the more and more shaky it becomes.

If you are a parent you will need this much courage – not to interfere. Open doors of unknown directions to the child so he can explore. He does not know what he has in him, nobody knows.

He has to grope in the dark. Don't make him afraid of darkness, don't make him afraid of failure, don't make him afraid of the unknown. Give him support. When he is going on an unknown journey, send him with all your support, with all your love, with all your blessings.

Don't let him be affected by your fears.

You may have fears, but keep them to yourself. Don't unload those fears on the child because that will be interfering.

After seven years, the next circle of seven years, from seven to fourteen, is a new addition to life: the child's first stirring of sexual energies. But they are only a kind of rehearsal.

To be a parent is a difficult job, so unless you are ready to take that difficult job, don't become a parent. People simply go on becoming fathers and mothers not knowing what they are doing. You are bringing a life into existence; all the care in the world will be needed.

Now when the child starts playing his sexual rehearsals, that is the time when parents interfere the most, because they have been interfered with. All that they know is what has been done to them, so they simply go on doing that to their children.

Societies don't allow sexual rehearsal, at least have not allowed it up to this century – only within the last two, three decades, and that too only in very advanced countries. Now children are having co-education. But in a country like India, even now co-education starts only at the university level.

The seven-year-old boy and the seven-year-old girl cannot be in the same boarding school. And this is the time for them – without any risk, without the girl getting pregnant, without any problems arising for their families – this is the time when they should be allowed all playfulness.

Yes, it will have a sexual color to it, but it is rehearsal; it is not the real drama. And if you don't allow them even the rehearsal and then suddenly one day the curtain opens, and the real drama starts... And those people don't know what is going on; even a prompter is not there to tell them what to do. You have messed up their life completely.

Those seven years, the second circle in life, is significant as a rehearsal. They will meet, mix, play, become acquainted. And that will help humanity to drop almost ninety percent of perversions.

If the children from seven to fourteen are allowed to be together;

to swim together, to be naked before each other, ninety percent of perversions and ninety percent of pornography will simply disappear. Who will bother about it?

When a boy has known so many girls naked, what interest can a magazine like Playboy have for him? When a girl has seen so many boys naked, I don't see that there is any possibility of curiosity about the other; it will simply disappear. They will grow together naturally, not as two different species of animals.

Right now that's how they grow: two different species of animals. They don't belong to one mankind; they are kept separate. A thousand and one barriers are created between them so they cannot have any rehearsal of the sexual life which is going to come.

But the way children are brought up is almost butchering their whole life. Those seven years of sexual rehearsal are absolutely essential. Girls and boys should be together in schools, in hostels, in swimming pools and beds. They should rehearse for the life which is going to come; they have to get ready for it. And there is no danger, there is no problem if a child is given total freedom about his growing sexual energy and is not condemned, repressed – which is being done now.

A very strange world it is in which you are living. You are born of sex, you will live for sex, your children will be born out of sex – and sex is the most condemned thing, the greatest sin. And all the religions go on putting this crap in your mind.

These people all around the world are full of everything rotten that you can conceive, for the simple reason that they have not been allowed to grow in the natural way. They have not been allowed to accept themselves. They have all become ghosts. They are not authentically real people, they are only shadows of someone they could have been; they are only shadows.

The second circle of seven years is immensely important because it will prepare you for the coming seven years. If you have done the homework right, if you have played with your sexual energy just in the spirit of a sportsman – and at that time, that is the only spirit you will have – you will not become a pervert, a homosexual.

All kinds of strange things will not come to your mind because you are moving naturally with the other sex, the other sex is moving with you; there is no hindrance, and you are not doing anything wrong against anybody. Your conscience is clear because nobody has put into your conscience ideas of what is right, what is wrong: you are simply being whatever you are.

Then from fourteen to twenty-one your sex matures. And this is significant to understand: if the rehearsal has gone well, in the seven years when your sex matures a very strange thing happens that you may never have thought about, because you have not been given the chance. I said to you that the second seven years, from seven to fourteen, give you a glimpse of foreplay. The third seven years give you a glimpse of afterplay. You are still together with girls or boys, but now a new phase starts in your being: you start falling in love.

From Darkness to Light, Session 3
March 2, 1985

Teenage Revolution

Beloved Osho,
How can teenagers create a bridge to their parents?

First, the teenagers should be honest and true, whatever the consequence. They should say to their parents whatever their feeling is – not arrogantly, but humbly. They should not hide anything from their parents. That is what is making the gap: parents are hiding many things from the children, children are hiding many things from the parents, and the gap becomes bigger and bigger.

One day I went to my father and I told him, "I want to start smoking cigarettes."

He said, "What?"

I said, "You have to give me money for it because I don't want to steal. If you don't give me I will steal, but the responsibility will be yours. If you don't allow me to smoke, I will smoke but I will smoke in hiding. And you will be making me a thief; you will be making me hide things and not be honest and open. I see so many people smoking cigarettes that I want to taste. I want the best cigarettes available, and I will smoke the first cigarette before you."

He said, "This is strange, but your argument is right. If I prevent it, you will steal. If I prevent it you will still smoke, so my preventing you will create more criminal things in you. It hurts me. I don't want you to start smoking."

I said, "That is not the question. The desire has arisen in me seeing people smoking. I want to check whether it is worth it. If it is worth it, then you will have to supply me constantly with cigarettes. If it is not worth it, then I am finished with it. But I don't want to do anything until you refuse; then the whole responsibility is yours, because I don't want to feel guilty."

He had to purchase the best cigarettes possible in the town – reluctantly. My uncles, my grandfather, were saying, "What are you doing? This is not done." They insisted...

But he said, "I know this is not done, but you don't know him as much as I know him. He will do exactly what he is saying, and I respect his truthfulness, his honesty. He has made his plan completely clear to me: 'Don't force me and don't prevent me, because that will make me feel guilty.' "

I smoked the cigarette, coughed, tears came to my eyes; I could not even finish one cigarette, and I dropped it. I told my father, "This is finished. You need not worry now. But I want you to understand that I will tell you about anything I feel so there is no need to hide anything from you. And if I hide even from my father then who am I going to relate with? No, I don't want to create any gap between me and you."

And seeing that I dropped the cigarettes, tears came to his eyes.

He said, "Everybody was against it, but your sincerity forced me to bring the cigarettes." Otherwise, in India perhaps no father has ever offered cigarettes to the son; it is unheard of. Fathers don't even smoke in front of their sons so that the very idea of smoking does not arise.

Teenagers are in a very difficult situation. They are changing; they are leaving childhood behind and they are becoming youngsters. Every day new dimensions of life are opening for them. They are in a transformation. They need immense help from the parents.

But right now the situation is that they don't meet the parents at all. They live in the same house but they don't talk with each other because they cannot understand each other's language, they cannot understand each other's viewpoints. They meet only when the boy or the girl needs money; otherwise there is no meeting. The gap goes on becoming bigger; they become as much strangers as one can imagine.

This is really a calamity.

Teenagers should be encouraged to say everything to their parents without any fear. This is not only going to help the children, it is going to help the parents too.

Truth has a beauty of its own; honesty has a beauty of its own. When teenagers approach their parents with honesty, truth, sincerity, and just open their hearts, it triggers something in the parents to open their hearts also, because they are also burdened with many things which they want to say but cannot. The society prohibits, the religion prohibits, the tradition prohibits.

But if they see the teenagers being completely open and clean it will help them also to be open and clean. And the so-called, much-discussed generation gap can simply be dropped; it can evaporate on its own accord.

The most troublesome problem is about sex. The children should be able to say exactly what is going on in their minds; there is no need to hide anything, because whatsoever is going on in their minds is natural. They should ask the advice of the parents – What can be done? – they are in a troubled state, and they need help. And to whom can they go except their parents?

If any problem was there, I simply told my parents. And that's my suggestion: the teenagers should not hide anything from the parents, from the teachers... they should be absolutely sincere, and the gap will evaporate. And we need the gap to evaporate, because what kind of society is this? There is a gap between parents and children, there is a gap between husband and wife, there is a gap between teachers and the taught. There are only gaps and gaps all around.

Everybody is surrounded with all kinds of gaps as if all communication has broken down. This is not a society, this is not a commune – because there is no communication. Nobody can say the right thing, everybody is repressed. Everybody is suppressing his desires, and everybody is angry, and everybody is feeling lonely, frustrated.

We have created an angry generation; we have created philosophies of meaninglessness.

And the whole reason for all this is that children have lost contact with the parents. Children can do a tremendous job, and they have the courage to do it. Perhaps parents may not be able to do it; they are much too conditioned. The teenagers are young and fresh; just teach them to be sincere with their parents.

I made a contract with my father. I told him, "I want to make a contract."

He said, "About what?"

I said, "The contract is that if I say the truth you have to reward me, not to punish me. Because if you punish me, then next time I will not say the truth."

And that's how it is happening all over the world: truth is being punished, so then the person stops saying it. Then he starts lying because lying is rewarded.

So I said to him, "You can decide. If you want me to lie, I can lie... if that is what you are going to reward. But if you are ready to reward the truth, then I will say the truth – but you cannot punish me for it."

He said, "I accept the contract." It is a simple method. If you cannot expose yourself to your own father and mother... in this whole world everybody is more of a stranger than them. Your father and mother are also strangers, but they are the closest strangers, the most intimate strangers.

Expose yourself to them so no gap exists. This will help them also to be sincere with you. This is something to be remembered: that sincerity, honesty, truth, trigger in the other person also the same qualities.

Socrates Poisoned Again After 25 Centuries, Session 23
March 2, 1986

Who is Kidding Who?

Beloved Osho,
How can I be a good parent?

According to me, you can do only one thing with your children, and that is share your own life. Tell them that you have been conditioned by your parents, that you have lived within certain limits, according to certain ideals, and because of these limits and ideals you have missed life completely, and you don't want to destroy your children's life. You want them to be totally free – free of you, because to them you represent the whole past.

It needs guts and it needs immense love in a father, in a mother, to tell the children, "You need to be free of us. Don't obey us – depend on your own intelligence. Even if you go astray it is far better than to remain a slave and always remain right. It is better to commit mistakes on your own and learn from them, rather than follow somebody else and not commit mistakes. But then you are never going to learn anything except following – and that is poison, pure poison."

It is very easy if you love. Don't ask "how", because "how" means you are asking for a method, a methodology, a technique – and love is not a technique.

Love your children, enjoy their freedom. Let them commit mistakes, help them to see where they have committed a mistake. Tell them, "To commit mistakes is not wrong – commit as many mistakes as possible, because that is the way you will be learning more. But don't commit the same mistake again and again, because that makes you stupid."

So it is not going to be a simple answer from me. You will have to figure it out living with your children moment to moment, allowing them every possible freedom in small things.

This should be the principle: children should be helped to listen to their bodies, to listen to their own needs. The basic thing for parents is to guard the children from falling into a ditch. The function of their discipline is negative.

Remember the word "negative"... no positive programming but only a negative guarding – because children are children, and they can get into something which will harm them, cripple them. Then too don't order them not to go, but explain to them. Don't make it a point of obedience; still let them choose. You simply explain the whole situation.

Children are very receptive, and if you are respectful towards them they are ready to listen, ready to understand; then leave them with their understanding. And it is a question only of a few years in the beginning; soon they will be getting settled in their intelligence, and your guarding will not be needed at all. Soon they will be able to move on their own.

I can understand the fear of the parents that the children may go in a direction which they don't like – but that is your problem. Your children are not born for your likings and your dislikings. They have to live their life, and you should rejoice that they are living their life – whatever it is.

Whenever you follow your potential, you always become the best. Whenever you go astray from the potential, you remain mediocre.

The whole society consists of mediocre people for the simple reason that nobody is what he was destined to be – he is something else. And whatever he will do, he cannot be the best, and he cannot feel a fulfillment; he cannot rejoice.

So the work of the parents is very delicate, and it is precious, because the whole life of the child depends on it. Don't give any positive program – help him in every possible way that he wants.

The function of a father or a mother is great, because they are bringing a new guest into the world – who knows nothing, but who brings some potential in him. And unless his potential grows, he will remain unhappy.

No parents like to think of their children remaining unhappy; they want them to be happy. It is just that their thinking is wrong. They think if they become doctors, if they become professors, engineers, scientists, then they will be happy. They don't know! They can only be happy if they become what they have come to become. They can only become the seed that they are carrying within themselves.

So help in every possible way to give freedom, to give opportunities. Ordinarily, if a child asks a mother anything, without even listening to the child, to what he is asking, the mother simply says no. "No" is an authoritative word; "yes" is not. So neither father nor mother nor anybody else who is in authority wants to say yes – to any ordinary thing.

The child wants to play outside the house: "No!" The child wants to go out while it is raining and wants to dance in the rain: "No! You will get a cold." A cold is not a cancer, but a child who has been prevented from dancing in the rain, and has never been able again to dance, has missed something great, something really beautiful. A cold would have been worthwhile – and it is not that he will necessarily have a cold. In fact the more you protect him, the more he becomes vulnerable. The more you allow him, the more he becomes immune.

Parents have to learn to say yes. In ninety-nine cases when they ordinarily say no, it is for no other reason than simply to show authority. Everybody cannot become the president of the country, cannot have authority over millions of people. But everybody can become a husband, can have authority over his wife; every wife can become a mother, can have authority over the child; every child can have a teddy bear, and have authority over the teddy bear... kick him from this corner to the other corner, give him good slaps, slaps that he really wanted to give to the mother or to father. And the poor teddy bear has nobody below him.

This is an authoritarian society.

What I am saying is in creating children who have freedom, who have heard "yes" and have rarely heard "no", the authoritarian society will disappear. We will have a more human society.

Beyond Psychology, Session 23
April 23, 1986

PART III
A NEW TOMORROW

The Family: Prisoners of Love

Beloved Osho,
The family has been the basic social unit for thousands of
years, yet you doubt its validity in your new world. What
do you suggest can replace it?

Man has outgrown the family. The utility of the family is finished;
it has lived too long. It is one of the most ancient institutions, so
only very perceptive people can see that it is dead already. It will
take time for others to recognize the fact that the family is dead.

It has done its work. It is no longer relevant in the new context
of things; it is no longer relevant for the new humanity that is just
being born.

The family has been good and bad. It has been a help – man
has survived through it -- and it has been very harmful because
it has corrupted the human mind. But there was no alternative in
the past, there was no way to choose anything else. It was a necessary
evil. That need not be so in the future. The future can have alternative
styles.

My idea is that the future is not going to be one fixed pattern,
it will have many, many alternative styles. If a few people still choose
to have a family, they should have the freedom to have it. It will
be a very small percentage. There are families on the earth – very
rare, not more than one per cent – which are really beautiful, which
are really beneficial, in which growth happens; in which there is
no authority, no power trip, no possessiveness; in which children
are not destroyed, in which the wife is not trying to destroy the

68

husband and the husband is not trying to destroy the wife; where love is and freedom is; where people have gathered together just out of joy – not for other motives; where there is no politics. Yes, these kind of families have existed on the earth; they are still there. For these people there is no need to change. In the future they can continue to live in families.

But for the great majority, the family is an ugly thing. You can ask the psychoanalysts and they will say, "All kinds of mental disease arise out of the family. All kinds of psychoses, neuroses arise out of the family." The family creates a very, very ill human being.

There is no need; alternative styles should be possible. For me, one alternative style is the commune – it is the best.

A commune means people living in a liquid family. Children belong to the commune, they belong to all. There is no personal property, no personal ego. A man lives with a woman because they feel like living together, because they cherish it, they enjoy it. The moment they feel that love is no longer happening, they don't go on clinging to each other. They say good-bye with all gratitude, with all friendship. They start moving with other people. The only problem in the past was what to do with the children. In a commune, children can belong to the commune, and that will be far better. They will have more opportunities to grow with many more kinds of people. Otherwise a child grows up with the mother. For years the mother and the father are the only two images of human beings for him. Naturally he starts imitating them. Children turn out to be imitators of their fathers, and they perpetuate the same kind of illness in the world as their parents did. They become ditto copies. It is very destructive. And there is no way for the children to do something else, they don't have any other source of information.

If a hundred people live together in a commune there will be many male members, many female members; the child need not get fixed and obsessed with one pattern of life. He can learn from his father, he can learn from his uncles, he can learn from all the men in the community. He will have a bigger soul.

Families crush people and give them very little souls. In the community the child will have a bigger soul, he will have more possibilities, he will be far more enriched in his being. He will see many women; he will not have one idea of a woman. It is very destructive to have only one single idea of a woman – because throughout your whole life you will be searching and searching for your mother. Whenever you fall in love with a woman, watch! There is every possibility that you have found someone that is similar to your mother, and that may be the thing that you should have avoided.

Each child is angry with his mother. The mother has to prohibit many things, the mother has to say no – it cannot be avoided. Even a good mother sometimes has to say no, and restrict and deny. The child feels rage, anger. He hates the mother and loves the mother also, because she is his survival, his source of life and energy. So he hates the mother and loves the mother together. And that becomes the pattern. You will love the woman and you will hate the same woman. And you don't have any other kind of choice. You will always go on searching, unconsciously, for your mother. And that happens to women also, they go on searching for their father. Their whole life is a search to find dad as a husband.

Now your dad is not the only person in the world; the world is far richer. And in fact, if you can find the dad you will not be happy. You can be happy with a beloved, with a lover, not with your daddy. If you can find your mother you will not be happy with her. You know her already, there is nothing else to explore. That is familiar already, and familiarity breeds contempt. You should search for something new, but you don't have any image.

In a commune a child will have a richer soul. He will know many women, he will know many men; he will not be addicted to one or two persons.

The family creates an obsession in you, and the obsession is against humanity. If your father is fighting with somebody and you see he is wrong, that doesn't matter – you have to be with the father and on his side. Just as people say, "Wrong or right, my country is my country!" so they say, "My father is my father, wrong or right. My mother is my mother, I have to be with her." Otherwise it will be a betrayal.

It teaches you to be unjust. You can see your mother is wrong and she is fighting with the neighbor and the neighbor is right –

but you have to be with the mother. This is learning an unjust life.

In a commune you will not be attached too much to one family – there will be no family to be attached to. You will be more free, less obsessed; you will be more just. And you will have love from many sources; you will feel that life is loving. The family teaches you a kind of conflict with society, with other families. The family demands monopoly; it asks you to be for it and against all. You have to be in the service of the family. You have to go on fighting for the name and the fame of the family. The family teaches you ambition, conflict, aggression. In a commune you will be less aggressive, you will be more at ease with the world because you have known so many people.

That's what I am going to create here – a commune, where all will be friends. Even husbands and wives should not be more than friends. Their marriage should be just an agreement between the two – that they have decided to be together because they are happy together. The moment even one of them decides that unhappiness is settling, then they separate. There is no need for any divorce. Because there is no marriage, there is no divorce. One lives spontaneously.

When you live miserably, by and by you become habituated to misery. Never for a single moment should one tolerate any misery. It may have been good to live with a man in the past, and joyful, but if it is no longer joyful then you have to get out of it. And there is no need to get angry and destructive, and there is no need to carry a grudge – because nothing can be done about love. Love is like a breeze. You see... it just comes. If it is there it is there. Then it is gone. And when it is gone it is gone. Love is a mystery, you cannot manipulate it. Love should not be manipulated, love should not be legalized, love should not be forced – for no reason at all.

In a commune, people will be living together just out of the sheer joy of being together, for no other reason. And when the joy has disappeared, they part. Maybe it feels sad, but they have to part. Maybe the nostalgia of the past still lingers in the mind, but they have to part. They owe it to each other that they should not live in misery, otherwise misery becomes a habit. They part with heavy hearts, but with no grudge. They will seek other partners.

In the future there will be no marriage as it has been in the past, and no divorce as it has been in the past. Life will be more liquid, more trusting. There will be more trust in the mysteries of life than in the clarities of the law, more trust in life itself than in anything – the court, the police, the priest, the church. And the children should belong to all – they should not carry the badges of their family. They will belong to the commune; the commune will take care of them.

This will be the most revolutionary step in human history – for people to start living in communes and to start being truthful, honest, trusting, and to go on dropping the law more and more.

In a family, love disappears sooner or later. In the first place it may not have been there at all from the very beginning. It may have been an arranged marriage – for other motives, for money, power, prestige. There may not have been any love from the very beginning. Then children are born out of a wedlock which is more like a deadlock – children are born out of no love. From the very beginning they become deserts. And this no-love state in the house makes them dull, unloving..They learn their first lesson of life from their parents, and the parents are unloving and there is constant jealousy and fighting and anger. And the children go on seeing the ugly faces of their parents.

Their very hope is destroyed. They can't believe that love is going to happen in their life if it has not happened in their parents' life. And they see other parents also, other families also. Children are very perceptive; they go on looking all around and observing. When they see that there is no possibility of love, they start feeling that love is only in poetry, it exists only for poets, visionaries – it has no actuality in life. And once you have learned the idea that love is just poetry, then it will never happen because you have become closed to it.

To see it happen is the only way to let it happen later on in your own life. If you see your father and mother in deep love, in great love, caring for each other, with compassion for each other, with respect for each other – then you have seen love happening.

Hope arises. A seed falls into your heart and starts growing. You know it is going to happen to you too.

If you have not seen it, how can you believe it is going to happen to you too? If it didn't happen to your parents, how can it happen to you? In fact, you will do everything to prevent it happening to you – otherwise it will look like a betrayal of your parents. This is my observation of people: women go on saying deep in the unconscious, "Look, Mom, I am suffering as much as you suffered." Boys go on saying to themselves later on, "Dad, don't be worried, my life is as miserable as yours. I have not gone beyond you, I have not betrayed you. I remain the same miserable person as you were. I carry the chain, the tradition. I am your representative, Dad, I have not betrayed you. Look, I am doing the same thing as you used to do to my mother – I am doing it to the mother of my children. And what you used to do to me, I am doing to my children. I am bringing them up in the same way you brought me up."

Each generation goes on giving its neurosis to the new people that come to the earth. And the society persists with all its madness, misery.

No, a different kind of thing is needed now. Man has come of age and the family is a thing of the past; it really has no future. The commune will be the thing that can replace the family, and it will be far more beneficial.

But in a commune only meditative people can be together. Only when you know how to celebrate life can you be together; only when you know that space I call meditation can you be together, can you be loving. The old nonsense of monopolizing love has to be dropped, then only can you live in a commune. If you go on carrying your old ideas of monopoly – that your woman should not hold somebody else's hand and your husband should not laugh with anybody else – if you carry these nonsensical things in your mind then you cannot become part of a commune.

If your husband is laughing with somebody else, it is good. Your husband is laughing – laughter is always good, with whom it happens it doesn't matter. Laughter is good, laughter is a value. If your woman is holding somebody else's hand... good. Warmth is flowing

– the flow of warmth is good, it is a value. With whom it is happening is immaterial. And if it is happening to your woman with many people, it will go on happening with you too. If it has stopped happening with anybody else, then it is going to stop with you too. The whole old idea is so stupid!

It is as if the moment your husband goes out, you say to him, "Don't breathe anywhere else. When you come home you can breathe as much as you want, but only when you are with me can you breathe. Outside hold your breath, become a yogi. I don't want you to breathe anywhere else." Now this looks stupid. But then why should love not be like breathing. Love is breathing.

Breathing is the life of the body and love is the life of the soul. It is far more important than breathing. Now when your husband goes out, you make it a point that he should not laugh with anybody else, not at least with any other woman. He should not be loving to anybody else. So for twenty-three hours he is unloving, then for one hour when he is in bed with you, he pretends to love. You have killed his love. It is flowing no more. If for twenty-three hours he has to remain a yogi, holding his love, afraid, do you think he can relax suddenly for one hour? It is impossible. You destroy the man, you destroy the woman, and then you are fed-up, bored. Then you start feeling, "He does not love me!" And it is you who created the whole thing. And then he starts feeling that you don't love him, and you are no longer as happy as you used to be before.

When people meet on a beach, when they meet in a garden, when they are on a date, nothing is settled and everything is liquid; both are very happy. Why? Because they are free. The bird on the wing is one thing, and the same bird in a cage is another thing. They are happy because they are free.

Man cannot be happy without freedom, and your old family structure destroyed freedom. And because it destroyed freedom it destroyed happiness, it destroyed love. It has been a kind of survival measure. Yes, it has somehow protected the body, but it has destroyed the soul. Now there is no need for it. We have to protect the soul too. That is far more essential and far more important.

There is no future for the family, not in the sense that it has been understood up to now. There is a future for love and love relationships. 'Husband' and 'wife' are going to become ugly and dirty words.

And whenever you monopolize the woman or the man, naturally you monopolize the children also. I agree totally with Thomas Gordon. He says, "I think all parents are potential child-abusers, because the basic way of raising children is through power and authority. I think it is destructive when many parents have the idea: 'It is my kid, I can do what I want to do with my kid.' It is violent, it is destructive to have the idea: 'It is my kid and I can do whatsoever I want with it.'" A kid is not a thing, it is not a chair, is not a car. You cannot do whatsoever you want to do with him. He comes through you but he does not belong to you. He belongs to God, to existence. You are at the most a caretaker; don't become possessive.

But the whole family idea is one of possession – possess property, possess the woman, possess the man, possess children – and possessiveness is poison. Hence, I am against the family. But I am not saying that those who are really happy in their families – flowing, alive, loving – have to destroy it. No, there is no need. Their family is already a commune, a small commune.

And of course a bigger commune will be far better, with more possibilities, more people. Different people bring different songs, different people bring different life-styles, different people bring different breathings, different breezes, different people bring different rays of light – and children should be showered with as many different life-styles as possible, so they can choose, so they can have the freedom to choose.

And they should be enriched by knowing so many women that they are not obsessed by the mother's face or the mother's style. Then they will be able to love many more women, many more men. Life will be more of an adventure.

I have heard...

A mother visiting a department store took her son to the toy department. Spying a gigantic rocking-horse, he climbed upon it and rocked back and forth for almost an hour.

"Come on, son," the mother pleaded, "I have to go home to

get father's dinner." The little lad refused to budge and all her efforts were unavailing. The department manager also tried to coax the little fellow, without meeting with any success. Eventually, in desperation, they called for the store psychiatrist.

Gently he walked over and whispered a few words in the boy's ear, and immediately the lad jumped off and ran to his mother's side.

"How did you do it?" the mother asked incredulously. "What did you say to him?"

The psychiatrist hesitated for a moment, then said, "All I said was, 'If you don't jump off that rocking-horse at once, son, I will knock the stuffing out of you!'"

People learn sooner or later that fear works, that authority works, that power works. And children are so helpless and they are so dependent on the parents that you can make them afraid. It becomes your technique to exploit them and oppress them, and they have nowhere to go.

In a commune they will have many places to go. They will have many uncles and many aunts and many people – they will not be so helpless. They will not be in your hands as much as they are right now. They will have more independence, less helplessness. You will not be able to coerce them so easily.

And all that they see in the home is misery. Sometimes, yes I know, sometimes the husband and wife are loving, but whenever they are loving it is always in private. Children don't know about it. Children see only the ugly faces, the ugly side. When the mother and the father are loving, they are loving behind closed doors. They keep quiet, they never allow the children to see what love is. The children see only their conflict – nagging, fighting, hitting each other, in gross and subtle ways, insulting each other, humiliating each other. Children go on seeing what is happening.

A man is sitting in his living room reading the newspaper when his wife comes over and slaps him.

"What was that for?" asked the indignant husband.

"That is for being a lousy lover."

A little while later the husband goes over to where the wife is sitting watching TV and he gives her a resounding smack.

"What was that for?" she yelled at him.

To which he answered, "For knowing the difference."

This goes on and on, and the children go on watching what is happening. Is this life? Is this what life is meant for? Is this all there is? They start losing hope. Before they enter into life they are already failures, they have accepted failure. If their parents who are so wise and powerful cannot succeed, what hope is there for them? It is impossible.

And they have learned the tricks – tricks of being miserable, tricks of being aggressive. Children never see love happening. In a commune there will be more possibilities. Love should come out into the open a little more. People should know that love happens. Small children should know what love is. They should see people caring for each other.

The idea is that you can fight in public but you cannot be loving in public. Fight is okay. You can murder, that is allowed. In fact, when two persons are fighting, a crowd will stand there to see what is happening. And everybody will enjoy it. That's why people go on reading and enjoying murder stories, suspense stories, detective stories. Murder is allowed, love is not allowed. If you are loving in public it is thought to be obscene. Now this is absurd. Love is obscene and murder is not obscene? Lovers are not to be loving in public and generals can go on walking in public showing all their medals – these are the murderers and these medals are for murder! Those medals show how much they have murdered, how many people they have killed. That is not obscene.

That should be the obscene thing. Nobody should be allowed to fight in public. It is obscene; violence is obscene. How can love be obscene? But love is thought to be obscene. You have to hide it in darkness. You have to make love so nobody knows. You have to make it so silently, so stealthily... naturally you can't enjoy it much. And people don't become aware of what love is. Children, particularly, have no way of knowing what love is.

In a better world, with more understanding, love will be there all over. Children will see what caring is. Children will see what joy it brings when you care for somebody. You can see it happening here. You can see little Siddhartha holding a girl's hand in a great caring, in great love. If they watch, they learn. If they know it happens, their doors open.

Love should be accepted more, violence should be rejected more. Love should be available more. Two persons making love should not be worried that no one should know. They should laugh, they should sing, they should scream in joy, so that the whole neighborhood knows that somebody is being loving to somebody – somebody is making love.

Love should be such a gift. Love should be so divine. It is sacred.

You can publish a book about a man being killed; that's okay, that is not pornography. To me, that is pornography. You cannot publish a book about a man lovingly holding a woman in deep, naked embrace – that is pornography. This world has existed against love up till now. Your family is against love, your society is against love, your state is against love. It is a miracle that love has still remained a little, it is unbelievable that love still goes on – not as it should be, it is just a small drop not an ocean – but that it has survived so many enemies is a miracle. It has not been destroyed completely – it is a miracle.

My vision of a commune is of loving people living together, with no antagonism towards each other, with no competition with each other, with love that is fluid, more available, with no jealousy and no possession. And the children will belong to all because they belong to God – everybody takes care of them. And they are such beautiful people, these children, who will not take care of them? And they have so many possibilities to see so many people loving, and each person loves in his own way, each woman loves in her own way – let the children see, play, enjoy. While their parents are making love, let them be there, let them be a part of it. Let them watch what happens to their mother when she makes love – how ecstatic her face becomes, what glow comes to her face, how her eyes close and she goes deep into herself; how their father becomes orgasmic, how he screams with joy. Let the children know!

Let the children know many people loving. They will become more rich. And I tell you that if these children exist in the world, none of them will read Playboy. There will be no need. Nude and naked pictures will disappear. They simply show starved sex, starved love.

The world will become almost non-sexual, it will be so loving. Your priest and your policeman have created all kinds of obscenity in the world. They are the source of all that is ugly. And your family has played a great part. The family has to disappear. It has to disappear into a bigger vision of a commune, of a life not based on small identities, more floating.

If families disappear, churches will disappear automatically, because families belong to churches. In a commune, there will be all kinds of people, all kinds of religion, all kinds of philosophies floating around, and the child will have the opportunity to learn. One day he goes with one uncle to the church, another day he goes with another uncle to the temple, and he learns all that is there and he can have a choice. He can choose and decide to what religion he would like to belong. Nothing is imposed.

Life can become a paradise here and now. The barriers have to be removed. The family is one of the greatest barriers.

Sufis: The People of the Path, Volume 2, Session 12
September 7, 1977

Genes Don't Have to Be Blue

Beloved Osho,
I still study in school and I want to know: What is the
secret of education?

It may be a little difficult for you to understand the secret of education. But I cannot come down from my vision, so I will tell what I feel is the secret, knowing perfectly well perhaps you may not be able to understand it yet, since you are too young. But through you perhaps others may understand, and one day you will also grow up and be in a position to understand it.

The question is very complex and I can see that you have asked it without knowing its implications. It is the question that is one of the most fundamental for the future of man. I would like to begin from the very beginning.

Up to now, man has been living an accidental life. No one knows what your potential is, what you are supposed by nature to be. And the question – the secret of education – cannot be decided without knowing what your potential is. Are you going to become a musician? a poet? an engineer? a doctor? Without knowing anything about your possibilities, almost groping in the dark, we go on deciding people's destiny for strange reasons.

The very word education, in its roots, means to draw out. It has the very secret in its root-meaning. Whatever is within you as a seed has to be drawn out, given full opportunity, so that it can blossom. But no one knows what is hidden within you, what kind of soil you need and what kind of gardener, what is the right climate and the right season and the right time for you to be sown.

Parents decide about their children according to their own ambitions.

Hence the immense misery in the world: the person who could have been a great musician has become just a pygmy industrialist. A person who could have been a great mystic has been forced to become a mathematician. Almost everybody is in the wrong place. And to be in the wrong place is very painful. You yourself are not aware of why you are suffering, because you yourself are not aware that you have missed your target. You are following somebody else's idea of what you should be.

So the first thing, according to me, begins with genetic engineering. There lies the secret of all education. Up to now what we have been calling education is a chaos.

The secret is in genetic engineering. Now it is scientifically possible to find the program of each human being, even before his birth. The male sperm carries many of the programs for his life and what he can become; whether he will be male or female, whether he will be a strong-bodied man or a weakling, whether he will live a life of health or will remain continually sick, his resistance against disease, how long he will live... and what kinds of potentialities are hidden in him – whether he can become a great mathematician or a great painter or a great poet or a great industrialist. Your destiny is written in the biological beginnings of your life, not in the birth-chart, nor in the stars, nor in the lines of your hands.

Now there are scientific openings to a new world: each sperm can be read almost like an open book. You can decide your child's life. Before he is born, you can choose what you want your child to be. To me, the real education begins from there.

In each lovemaking the man releases at least one million sperms, but only one sperm may be able to reach the female egg. It is a marathon race. The small sperm – which is not visible to the bare eyes – in proportion to his size, the track that he has to follow towards the mother's egg is almost two miles long, and he has only two hours' lifespan. So if he does not reach within two hours, he will die. Such competition he will never again face in his life.

The whole life will be competitive, but the beginning is the worst competition you can conceive: one million people rushing towards the female egg, and only one is going to win the race! The remainder are going to die.

Now it is a blind game – most probably the idiots will reach first. That's why the world is full of idiots! The idiots will not take any care, any consideration of anybody; they will simply rush blindly with full force. The wiser ones may stand by the side and see what is happening. The really wise ones may not even participate in the race, it is so stupid.

These problems can be solved. But religious superstitiousness is a great barrier in the world for every kind of progress and new idea.

I will be opposed by all the religions – it does not matter, I have been opposed my whole life – but my proposal is that every male who wants children should donate his sperms to a hospital and the medical science board should work out for those sperms what the possibilities are.

In those one million sperms there may be Albert Einsteins, Bertrand Russells, Martin Heideggers, great musicians like Yehudi Menuhin, great dancers like Nijinsky, great philosophers like Friedrich Nietzsche, great novelists like Fyodor Dostoyevsky. They can be picked out and the father and mother can choose what they want. When you can choose the great diamonds, why go for the colored stones? And when you can be the chooser, why be accidental?

They can choose, if they want, a Henry Ford, who will make great riches possible. Money is an art, just as anything else; it has its own geniuses. Everybody cannot be a Henry Ford!

If you want your child to be a Gautam Buddha, then you have to see, according to the genetic analysis, which sperm has the potentiality of being a mystic. The sperm has to be injected, so he need not be in competition with all kinds of fellows in a crowd. From that choice starts your education.

This is only the beginning of genetic engineering. Finally it is going to happen, the work is growing every day... the chosen sperm has a program, but the program can be changed a little bit. It may be possible that he has the mind of an Albert Einstein, but not the body, not the health – that can be added, the program can be changed a little bit. He may have just a life of fifty years, but that program can be changed. He can be given as long a life as you want – the maximum lifespan can be almost three hundred years – and as much health and as much resistance against disease. All these things can be added to the program.

The child now starts the journey with the parents' full awareness of what he is going to become, to what school he should be sent, and what kind of education he should be given according to the genetic code. Then the world will be full of geniuses, talented people, healthy people. It is possible to avoid old age completely... a man can go on living youthfully up to the point of death.

Now these are not fictions, these have become scientific facts. But religions are even preventing these scientific facts from being known to the public, to the people. They are afraid of strange things. Their fear is that morality will be disturbed. So let it be disturbed...! Anyway, what kind of morality exists in the world? Except hypocrisy, there exists no morality.

Genetic engineering can decide even the character, the morality, the discipline of the individual who is going to be born. From there many things become possible. For the child, a clear-cut, non-accidental career, and for the parents – because the child is not be given birth through sex – sex becomes pure fun. It does not carry any responsibility, any danger.

The scientific truth is that people are unnecessarily suffering because we are listening to the priests and not to the scientists. The priests are absolutely against interfering as far as human life is concerned. They start great protests immediately that you should not interfere in the work of God.

But I cannot see what kind of work God is doing. All these people who are retarded, stupid – this is God's work? And the priests are not ready to have a different world. They are against family planning, they are against birth control, they are against everything that man is now capable of doing to create a better world, a better humanity.

So this is my first thing: education will never be right unless children are born through genetic engineering, not through the old bullock-cart method that you have followed up to now. This is one of the most significant secrets: unless we listen to sanity and intelligence, we are not going to revolutionize human life.

The Great Pilgrimage from Here to Here, Session 17
October 3, 1987

Five-dimensional Education

Beloved Osho,
Can You please explain Your vision of education?

The education that has prevailed in the past is very insufficient, incomplete, superficial. It only creates people who can earn their livelihood but it does not give any insight into living itself. It is not only incomplete, it is harmful too – because it is based on competition.

Any type of competition is violent deep down, and creates people who are unloving. Their whole effort is to be the achievers – of name, of fame, of all kinds of ambitions. Obviously they have to struggle and be in conflict for them. That destroys their joys and that destroys their friendliness. It seems everybody is fighting against the whole world.

Education up to now has been goal-oriented: what you are learning is not important; what is important is the examination that will come a year or two years later. It makes the future important – more important than the present. It sacrifices the present for the future. And that becomes your very style of life; you are always sacrificing the moment for something which is not present. It creates a tremendous emptiness in life.

The commune of my vision will have a five-dimensional education.

Before I enter into those five dimensions, a few things have to be noted. One: there should not be any kind of examination as part of education, but every day, every hour observation by the teachers; their remarks throughout the year will decide whether you move further or you remain a little longer in the same class.

Nobody fails, nobody passes – it is just that a few people are speedy and a few people are a little bit lazy – because the idea of failure creates a deep wound of inferiority, and the idea of being successful also creates a different kind of disease, that of superiority.

Nobody is inferior, and nobody is superior.

One is just oneself, incomparable.

So, examinations will not have any place. That will change the whole perspective from the future to the present. What you are doing right this moment will be decisive, not five questions at the end of two years. Of thousands of things you will pass through during these two years, each will be decisive; so the education will not be goal-oriented.

The teacher has been of immense importance in the past, because he knew he had passed all the examinations, he had accumulated knowledge. But the situation has changed – and this is one of the problems, that situations change but our responses remain the old ones. Now the knowledge explosion is so vast, so tremendous, so speedy, that you cannot write a big book on any scientific subject because by the time your book is complete, it will be out of date; new facts, new discoveries will have made it irrelevant. So now science has to depend on articles, on periodicals, not on books.

The teacher was educated thirty years earlier. In thirty years everything has changed, and he goes on repeating what he was taught. He is out of date, and he is making his students out of date. So in my vision the teacher has no place. Instead of teachers there will be guides, and the difference has to be understood: the guide will tell you where, in the library, to find the latest information on the subject.

And teaching should not be done in the old-fashioned way, because television can do it in a far better way, can bring the latest information without any problems. The teacher has to appeal to your ears; television appeals directly to your eyes; and the impact is far greater, because the eyes absorb eighty percent of your life situations – they are the most alive part.

If you can see something there is no need to memorize it; but if you listen to something you have to memorize it. Almost ninety-eight percent of education can be delivered through television, and the questions that students will ask can be answered by computers.

The teacher should be only a guide to show you the right channel, to show you how to use the computer, how to find the latest book. His function will be totally different. He is not imparting knowledge to you, he is making you aware of the contemporary knowledge, of the latest knowledge. He is only a guide.

With these considerations, I divide education into five dimensions.

The first is informative, like history, geography, and many other subjects which can be dealt with by television and computer together.

The second part should be sciences. They can be imparted by television and computer too, but they are more complicated, and the human guide will be more necessary.

In the first dimension also come languages. Every person in the world should know at least two languages; one is his mother tongue, and the other is English as an international vehicle for communication. They can also be taught more accurately by television – the accent, the grammar, everything can be taught more correctly than by human beings.

We can create in the world an atmosphere of brotherhood: language connects people and language disconnects too. There is right now no international language.

English is the most widespread language, and people should drop their prejudices – they should look at the reality. There have been many efforts to create languages to avoid the prejudices – the Spanish people can say their language should be the international language because it is spoken by more people than almost any other language... To avoid these prejudices, languages like Esperanto have been created.

But no created language has been able to function. There are a few things which grow, which cannot be created; a language is a growth of thousands of years. Esperanto looks so artificial that all those efforts have failed.

But it is absolutely necessary to create two languages – first, the mother tongue, because there are feelings and nuances which you can say only in the mother tongue. One of my professors, S. K. Saxena, a world traveler who has been a professor of philosophy in many countries, used to say that in a foreign language you can do everything, but when it comes to a fight or to love, you feel that you are not being true and sincere to your feelings. So for your feelings and for your sincerity, your mother tongue... which you imbibe with the milk of the mother, which becomes part of your blood and bones and marrow. But that is not enough – that creates small groups of people and makes others strangers.

One international language is absolutely necessary as a basis for one world, for one humanity. So two languages should be absolutely necessary for everybody. That will come in the first dimension.

The second is the enquiry of scientific subjects, which is tremendously important because it is half of reality, the outside reality. And the third will be what is missing in present-day education, the art of living. People have taken it for granted that they know what love is. They don't know... and by the time they know, it is too late. Every child should be helped to transform his anger, hatred, jealousy, into love.

An important part of the third dimension should also be a sense of humor. Our so-called education makes people sad and serious. And if one third of your life is wasted in a university in being sad and serious, it becomes ingrained; you forget the language of laughter – and the man who forgets the language of laughter has forgotten much of life.

So love, laughter, and an acquaintance with life and its wonders, its mysteries... these birds singing in the trees should not go unheard. The trees and the flowers and the stars should have a connection with your heart. The sunrise and the sunset will not be just outside things – they should be something inner, too. A reverence for life should be the foundation of the third dimension.

People are so irreverent to life.

They still go on killing animals to eat – they call it game; and if the animal eats them – then they call it calamity. Strange... in a game both parties should be given equal opportunity. The animals are without weapons and you have machine guns or arrows.

A great reverence for life should be taught, because life is God and there is no other God than life itself, and joy, laughter, a sense of humor – in short a dancing spirit.

The fourth dimension should be of art and creativity: painting, music, craftsmanship, pottery, masonry – anything that is creative. All areas of creativity should be allowed; the students can choose. There should be only a few things compulsory – for example an international language should be compulsory; a certain capacity to earn your livelihood should be compulsory; a certain creative art should be compulsory. You can choose through the whole rainbow of creative arts, because unless a man learns how to create, he never becomes a part of existence, which is constantly creative. By being creative one becomes divine; creativity is the only prayer.

And the fifth dimension should be the art of dying. In this fifth dimension will be all the meditations, so that you can know there is no death, so that you can become aware of an eternal life inside you. This should be absolutely essential, because everybody has to die; nobody can avoid it. And under the big umbrella of meditation, you can be introduced to Zen, to Tao, to Yoga, to Hassidism, to all kinds and all possibilities that have existed, but which education has not taken any care of. In this fifth dimension, you should also be made aware of the martial arts like aikido, jujitsu, judo – the art of self-defense without weapons – and not only self-defense, but simultaneously a meditation too.

The new commune will have a full education, a whole education. All that is essential should be compulsory, and all that is nonessential should be optional. One can choose from the options, which will be many. And once the basics are fulfilled, then you have to learn something you enjoy; music, dance, painting – you have to know something to go inwards, to know yourself. And all this can be done very easily without any difficulty. I have been a professor myself and I resigned from the university with a note saying: This is not education, this is sheer stupidity; you are not teaching anything significant.

But this insignificant education prevails all over the world – it makes no difference, in the Soviet Union or in America. Nobody has looked for a more whole, a total education. In this sense almost everybody is uneducated; even those who have great degrees are uneducated in the vaster areas of life. A few are more uneducated, a few are less – but everybody is uneducated. But to find an educated man is impossible, because education as a whole does not exist anywhere.

The Golden Future, Session 23
May 23, 1987

Teaching: A Put Down or A Lift Up

Beloved Osho,
You often tell us that we should not judge ourselves or
other people. I am a teacher and because of my job I have
to judge the students. Now I am worried about how I shall
manage with my job. Can you give me some help?

My saying that you should not judge does not mean that you cannot say to a student, because you are a teacher, "The answer you have brought is not right."

It is not judging the person, it is judging the act. And I am not telling you not to judge the act – that is a totally different thing.

For example, somebody is a thief – you can judge that stealing is not good. But don't judge the person, because the person is a vast phenomenon, and the act is a small thing. The act is so small a piece... that small piece should not become a judgment about the whole person. A thief may have many beautiful values; he may be truthful, he may be sincere, he may be a very loving person.

But most often what happens is just the opposite: people start judging the person rather than the action. Actions have to be corrected – and particularly in a profession like teaching, you have to correct; you cannot allow students to go on doing wrong things. That will be very cruel, uncompassionate.

But don't correct them according to tradition, convention, according to so-called morality, according to your prejudices. Whenever you are correcting somebody, be very meditative, be very silent; look at the whole thing from all perspectives. Perhaps it is the right thing that they are doing, and your prevention will not be right at all.

So when I say, "Don't judge," I simply mean that no action gives you the right to condemn the person. If the action is not right, help the person – find out why the action is not right, but there is no question of judgment. Don't take the person's dignity, don't humiliate him, don't make him feel guilty – that's what I mean when I say, "Don't judge."

But as far as correcting is concerned: unprejudiced, silently, in your awareness, if you see that something is wrong and will destroy that person's intelligence, will take him on the wrong paths in his life, help him.

The job of the teacher is not just to teach futile things – geography, and history, and all kinds of nonsense. His basic function is to bring the students to a better consciousness, to a higher consciousness. This should be your love and your compassion, and this should be the only value on which you judge any action as right or wrong.

But never for a single moment let the person feel that he has been condemned. On the contrary, let him feel that he has been loved – it is out of love that you have tried to correct him.

A guy lying in a hospital bed, coming around from an anesthetic, wakes up to find the doctor sitting beside him.

"I have got bad news and good news for you," says the doctor, "would you like the bad or good first?"

"Aaagh," groans the guy, "tell me the bad."

"Well," says the doctor. "We had to amputate both your legs above the knee."

"Aaagh," groans the guy, "that's really bad."

After recovering from the shock, he asks the doctor for the good news.

"Well," said the doctor, "the man in the next bed would like to buy your slippers!"

Just don't be serious! Don't think that you are a teacher so you are in a very serious job. Look at life with more playful eyes... it is really hilarious! There is nothing to judge – everybody is doing his best. If you feel disturbed by somebody, it is your problem, not his. First correct yourself.

The Invitation, Session 23
September 9, 1987

The Generation Gap: Mutual Disrespect

Beloved Osho,
What is this generation gap? I hear so much about it
these days.

Two old men of eighty were sitting in their club when one said, "Do you think there is as much love, as much fun going on as there used to be?"

"Yes, certainly," said the other, "but there is a whole new bunch doing it."

That's what the generation gap is.

A large crowd had been waiting quietly at the foot of a mountain. Moses had been gone for hours. Suddenly his white robe was seen fluttering in the breeze, and now the lawgiver stood before his flock: "People of Israel! I have been with the Lord for seven hours and I now have some good news, and some bad news..."

"Speak, O Moses!" shouted the crowd.

"The good news," says Moses, "is that I have managed to bring the number of commandments down to ten!"

The people cheered. Then they cried, "Moses, what is the bad news?"

Moses sadly replied, "Adultery is still in."

For the new generation it is no longer in. That's the generation gap. Now the whole meaning of adultery has changed: it simply means to be adult.

There has never been any generation gap in the past. Hence, one has to look deeply into it because this is the first time in the whole history of man that even the expression 'generation gap' has been used. And the gap is growing bigger and bigger every day. Things seem to be unbridgeable.

There is certainly a great psychology behind it. In the past there used to be no young age. You will be surprised to know about it: children used to become adult without being young. A six-year-old, seven-year-old child would start working with his father; if the father was a carpenter he would learn carpentry, or at least help his father. If the father was a farmer he would go to the farm with the father, would help him with the animals, cows, horses. By the age of six or seven he had already entered into life. By the age of twenty he would be married and have a few children.

In the past there was no 'younger generation' hence there was no gap. One generation followed another generation in a continuity, with no gap between them. By the time the father died, his son would have already replaced him in every field of his life. There was no time to play and there was no time to get educated; there were no schools, no colleges, no universities.

The new generation is a by-product of many things. In the past the only way of learning was to participate with the older generation, work with them – that was the only way to learn. And of course the older generation was always respected, because they were the teachers. They knew, and you were ignorant; the ignorant necessarily respected the knowledgeable. Hence in the past it was almost inconceivable that the younger people would disrespect the old people, or could even think in their dreams that they knew more than the older people. Knowledge was very decisive.

The people who knew had the power, and the people who did not, had no power. It was in those old days that the proverb must have been coined: "Knowledge is power." That was the only criterion in life, so you never heard of any revolt of the young against the old.

This generation has come to a new, totally new stage. The child never follows in his father's footsteps. He goes to the school; his father goes to his shop or to the office or to the farm. By the time he comes back from his university he is twenty-five years old. For these twenty-five years he has no connection with the older generation. His only connection is financial; they help him financially. In these twenty-five years many things happen: one, he knows more than his parents because his parents had been to school at least twenty, twenty-five years before. In these twenty-five years, knowledge has taken such quantum leaps – it has grown so much...

By learning, studying, you can know as much as you want. Just sitting in the library you can know the whole world in all its dimensions, whatsoever is happening. You need not even move out of the library.

And you are going to see a still bigger gap – one of which humanity is still not aware – and I am talking about it for the first time. One gap has been created by education. If meditation becomes a worldwide movement, another gap will be created which will be immense. Then the old man and the young man will be as far apart as the two poles of the earth. Even communication between them has already become difficult; it will become impossible.

The people who are here with me can understand what I am saying. If you start moving into the world of no-mind, then the people who are old, who have gathered much knowledge in the mind, will look to you retarded, undeveloped, very ordinary. There is no reason why you should respect them; they will have to respect you – you have transcended mind.

And the world is becoming more and more interested in meditation. It will not be long before that day when meditation will become your education for the ultimate. Your ordinary education is about the outside. Meditation will be the education about your interiority, about your inner being.

The generation gap is unfortunate. I am not in favor of it. I have my own strategy for how it can be avoided. The whole system of education has to be changed from the very roots. In short... we prepare people in education for livelihood rather than life. For twenty-five years we prepare – that is one third of the life – for livelihood. We never prepare people for death, and life is only seventy years; death is the door to eternity. It needs tremendous training.

According to me – and I feel with great authority that this is going to happen in the future if man survives – education should be cut into pieces: fifteen years for livelihood, and again after forty-two years, ten years in preparing for death. Education should be divided in two parts. Everybody goes to the university – of course to different universities, or to the same university but to different departments. One is to prepare children for life and one is to prepare people who have lived life and now want to know something more, beyond life.

Then the generation gap will disappear. Then the people who are of an older age will be more quiet, more silent, more peaceful, more wise; their advice will be worth listening to.

The second part of education should consist of meditativeness, of awareness, of witnessing, of love, of compassion, of creativity – and certainly we will again be without any generation gap. The younger person will respect the older person, and not for any formal reasons but actually because the old person is respectable. He knows something beyond the mind and the young person knows only something within the mind.

The young person is still struggling in the trivia of the world, and the older person has gone beyond the clouds; he has almost reached to the stars. It is not a question of etiquette to respect him. You are bound to respect him, it is absolutely a compulsion of your own heart – not a formality taught by others.

Old people should behave like enlightened people – not only behave, they should be enlightened. They should become a light to those who are still young and under biological infatuations, natural bondages. They have gone beyond; they can become guiding stars.

When education for death and education for livelihood are separated, when everybody goes twice to the university – first to learn how to go around this world of trivia and the second time to learn about eternity – the gap will disappear. And it will disappear in a beautiful way.

The Great Pilgrimage from Here to Here, Session 7
September 9, 1987

Meditation: Nature's Gift

Beloved Osho,
Surely, meditation is for mystics. Why do you propose it
for ordinary people and their children?

It is for mystics, surely, but everybody is a born mystic – because everybody carries a great mystery within him which has to be realized, everybody carries great potentiality which has to be actualized. Everybody is born with a future. Everybody has hope. What do you mean by a mystic? A mystic is one who is trying to realize the mystery of life, who is moving into the unknown, who is going into the uncharted, whose life is a life of adventure, exploration.

But every child starts that way – with awe, with wonder, with great enquiry in his heart. Every child is a mystic. Somewhere on the way of your so-called growing you lose contact with your inner possibility of being a mystic, and you become a businessman or you become a clerk or you become a civil servant or you become a minister. You become something else. And you start thinking that you are this. And when you believe it, it is so.

My effort here is to destroy your wrong notions about yourself and to liberate your mysticism. Meditation is a way of liberating the mysticism, and it is for everybody – without any exception, it knows no exception.

Surely meditation is for mystics. Why do you propose it for ordinary
people and their children?

Children are the most capable. They are natural mystics. And before they are destroyed by the society, before they are destroyed by other robots, by other corrupted people, it is better to help them to know something of meditation.

Meditation is not a conditioning because meditation is not indoctrination. Meditation is not giving them any creed. If you teach a child to become Christian you have to give him a doctrine; you have to force him to believe things which naturally look absurd. You have to tell the child that Jesus was born out of a virgin mother – that becomes a fundamental. Now you are destroying the natural intelligence of the child.

But if you teach a child meditation you are not indoctrinating him. You don't say he has to believe anything, you simply invite him to an experiment in no-thought. No-thought is not a doctrine, it is an experience. And children are very, very capable because they are very close to the source. They still remember something of that mystery. They have just come from the other world, they have not yet forgotten it completely. Sooner or later they will forget, but still the fragrance is around them. That's why all children look so beautiful, so graceful. Have you even seen an ugly child?

Then what happens to all these beautiful children? Where do they disappear to? Later in life it is very rare to find beautiful people. Then what happens to all the beautiful children? Why do they turn into ugly persons? What accident, what calamity happens on the way?

They start losing their grace the day they start losing their intelligence. They start losing their natural rhythm, their natural elegance and they start learning plastic behavior. They no longer laugh spontaneously, they no longer cry spontaneously, they no longer dance spontaneously. You have forced them into a cage, a strait-jacket. You have imprisoned them.

The chains are very subtle, they are not very visible. The chains are of thought – Christian, Hindu, Mohammedan. You have chained the child and he cannot see the chains, so he will not be able to see how he is chained. And he will suffer his whole life. It is such an imprisonment. It is not like throwing a man into a jail. It is creating a jail around a man, so wherever he goes the jail continues around him. He can go to the Himalayas and sit in a cave, and he will remain a Hindu, he will remain a Christian – and he will still think thoughts.

Meditation is a way to go within yourselves to that depth where thoughts don't exist, so it is not indoctrination. It is not teaching you anything, in fact, it is just making you alert to your inner capacity to be without thought, to be without mind. And the best time is when the child is still uncorrupted.

Sufis, The People of the Path, Volume I, Session 10
August 20, 1977

Conscious Innocence: Paradise Regained

Beloved Osho,
Why is childlikeness compared to meditation?

Man is reborn – only then he understands what is the beauty and the grandeur of childhood. The child is ignorant; hence he is unable to understand the tremendous innocence that surrounds him. Once a child becomes aware of his own innocence, there is no difference between the child and the sage. The sage is not higher and the child is not lower. The only difference is, the child knows not what he is and the sage knows it.

I am reminded of Socrates. In his very last moments of life he said to his disciples, "When I was young I used to think I knew much. As I became older, as I knew more, a strange thing started happening, an awareness that knowing more is bringing me to knowing less."

And finally, when the Oracle of Delphi declared Socrates to be the wisest man in the world... the people of Athens were very happy and they went to Socrates, but Socrates said, "Go back and tell the Oracle that at least for once its prophecy has been wrong. Socrates knows nothing."

The people were shocked. They went to the Oracle... but the Oracle laughed and he said, "That's why I have declared him the wisest man in the world! It is only the ignorant people who think they know." The more you know, the more you become innocent.

According to the Socratic division, there are two categories of people: the ignorant knowers and the knowing ignorants. The world is dominated by the second category. These are your priests, your professors; these are your leaders, these are your saints, these are your religious messiahs, saviors, prophets, all proclaiming that they know. But their very proclamation destroys the utter simplicity and innocence of a child.

Bodhidharma remained in China for fourteen years. He was sent by his master to spread the message of meditation. After fourteen years, he wanted to come back to the Himalayas; he was old enough and was ready to disappear into the eternal snows. He had thousands of disciples – he was one of the rarest people who have existed on the earth – but he called only four disciples and he said, "I will ask only one question – what is the essence of my teaching? Whoever gives me the right answer will be my successor."

There was great silence, tremendous expectation. Everybody looked at the first disciple, who was the most learned, most scholarly. The first disciple said, "Going beyond the mind is all that your teaching can be reduced to."

Bodhidharma said, "You have my skin, but not more than that."

He turned to the second disciple who said, "There is no one to go beyond the mind. All is silent. There is no division between the one that has to be transcended and one that has to transcend. This is the essence of your teaching."

Bodhidharma said, "You have my bones."

And he turned to the third disciple, who said, "The essence of your teaching is inexpressible."

Bodhidharma laughed and he said, "But you have expressed it! You have said something about it. You have my marrow."

And he turned to the fourth disciple who had only tears and utter silence, no answer. He fell at the feet of Bodhidharma... and he was accepted as the successor, although he had not answered anything.

But he has answered – without answering, without using words, without using language. His tears have shown much more than any language can contain. And his gratitude and his prayerfulness and his thankfulness to the master... what more can you say?

The great gathering of disciples were very much disappointed, because this was a man nobody had ever bothered about. The great scholars have been rejected; the great knowers have not been accepted, and an ordinary man...

But that ordinariness is the only extraordinary thing in the world... that childlike wonder, that childlike experience of the mysterious all around.

Remember one thing: the moment you start knowing something you are not a child. You have started becoming part of the adult world. The society has initiated you into civilization; it has distracted you from your essential nature.

When the child is surrounded by the mysterious all around, everything just a mystery with no answer, with no question, he is exactly at the point the sage ultimately reaches. That's why child-likeness is compared again and again to meditation. Meditation would not have been needed if people had remained in their essential childlikeness.

Do you know the root of the word meditation? – it comes from the same root as medicine. It is a medicine. But the medicine is needed only if you are sick. Meditation is needed if you are spiritually sick. Childlikeness is your spiritual health, your spiritual wholeness; you don't need any meditation.

Little Ernie wants a bicycle, but when he asks his mother, she tells him he can only have one if he behaves himself, which he promises to do. But after a week of trying to be good, Ernie finds it impossible. So his mother suggests, "If you write a note to Jesus, maybe you will find it easier to be good."

Ernie rushes upstairs, sits on his bed and writes: "Dear Jesus, if you let me have a bike, I promise to be good for the rest of my life." Realizing that he could never manage that, he starts again: "Dear Jesus, if you let me have a bike, I promise to be good for a month." Knowing that he can't do that, he suddenly has an idea.

He runs into his mother's room, takes her statue of the Virgin Mary, puts it in a shoe box and hides it under the bed. Then he begins to write again: "Dear Jesus, if you ever want to see your mother again... "

For absolutely irrational reasons, man has been dragged into seriousness. All religions have played their role in poisoning man.

The people who are going for any kind of power trip are bound to destroy man's laughter, his innocent wondering eyes, his childhood. The giggle of a child seems to be more dangerous to these people than nuclear weapons. And in fact they are right – if the whole world starts laughing a little more, wars will be reduced. If people start loving their innocence without bothering about knowledge, life will have a beauty and a blessing of which we have become completely unaware.

Om Mani Padme Hum, Session 3
December 22, 1987

The Mystic Rose Meditation for children

The whole of life has become just a utility: either you are an inspector, or you are a police commissioner, or you are a minister, or you are a teacher – just a function which any robot can do.

The only thing that the robot cannot do is meditation. In other words, I am saying that those who are not in meditation are being robots, without being aware that they are just utilities, functions, they are needed.

But a man of meditation for the first time realizes that it does not matter whether he is needed or not – he himself is a joy unto himself. He himself is bliss, he does not depend on anybody to make him blissful. That is the only freedom possible in the world. Otherwise everybody is a slave.

I want you to understand it absolutely that unless you become blissful on your own accord, unless your rose opens within your own being, you are just a commodity, just a thing, an object. Meditation reveals your subjectivity. Subjectivity is your consciousness, and your consciousness and its experience makes your life significant, meaningful, eternal, immortal, without any beginning and without any end. A celebration, moment to moment a dance.

And unless you have transformed your life into a moment-to-moment dance you have missed the opportunity that existence gives you.

Yaa-Hoo! The Mystic Rose

The following is a meditation suggested by Osho for children and their teachers to do together at the beginning of each school day.

Stage 1
Ten minutes gibberish. With eyes closed, make any nonsense sounds you like; sing, cry, shout. Let your body do whatever it wants; jump, shake, walk, sit. Everything is allowed, go totally mad.

The word 'gibberish' comes from a Sufi mystic, Jabbar. Jabbar never spoke any language, he just uttered nonsense. Still he had thousands of disciples because what he was saying was, "Your mind is nothing but gibberish. Put it aside and you will have a taste of your own being."

To use gibberish, don't say things which are meaningful, don't use the language that you know. Use Chinese if you don't know Chinese. Use Japanese if you don't know Japanese. Don't use German if you know German. For the first time have a freedom – the same as all the birds have. Simply allow whatever comes to your mind without bothering about its rationality, reasonability, meaning, significance – just the way the birds are doing.

Live Zen

Stage 2
Ten minutes belly laughter with eyes open or closed.

Simply laugh for no reason at all. And whenever the laughter starts dying then say, "Yaa-Hoo!" and it will come back. Digging, you will be surprised how many layers of dust have gathered upon your being. It will cut them like a sword, in one blow... You cannot conceive how much transformation can come to your being...

The authentic laughter is not about anything. It is simply arising in you as a flower blossoms in a tree. It has no reason, no rational explanation. It is mysterious; hence the symbol of the mystic rose.

Yaa-Hoo! The Mystic Rose

Stage 3

Ten minutes silence with eyes closed, sitting or lying, just watching and witnessing your body, your surroundings, your thoughts, without any judgement.

Be silent, no movement... go in. Close your eyes. This is you. No portrait of it is possible. it is just a pure silence, a space without boundaries. This is all that you have brought into the world, and this is all that you will take away when you die. In birth, in life, in death, this is the only thing that constantly remains the same. The unchanging, ultimate truth.

To experience it go deeper and deeper. Drop all fear, because it is your own being, your own unknown territory that you are going to explore. There is no question of fear. Nobody else can enter there, it is absolutely private. Hence fearlessly open your wings, the whole sky is yours.

Zen, The Solitary Bird, Cuckoo of the Forest

ABOUT OSHO

MOST OF US live out our lives in the world of time, in memories of the past and anticipation of the future. Only rarely do we touch the timeless dimension of the present - in moments of sudden beauty, or sudden danger, in meeting with a lover or with the surprise of the unexpected. Very few people step out of the world of time and mind, its ambitions and competitiveness, and begin to live in the world of the timeless. And of those who do, only a few have attempted to share their experience. Lao Tzu, Gautama Buddha, Bodhidharma...or more recently, George Gurdjieff, Ramana Maharshi, J. Krishnamurti — they are thought by their contemporaries to be eccentrics or madmen; after their death they are called "philosophers". And in time they become legends — not flesh-and-blood human beings, but, perhaps, mythological representations of our collective wish to grow beyond the smallness and trivia, the meaninglessness of our everyday lives.

Osho is one who has discovered the door to living His life in the timeless dimension of the present — He has called Himself a "true existentialist" - and He has devoted His life to provoking others to seek this same door, to step out of the world of past and future and discover for themselves the world of eternity.

Osho was born in Kuchwad, Madhya Pradesh, India, on December 11, 1931. From His earliest childhood, His was a rebellious and independent spirit, insisting on experiencing the truth for Himself rather than acquiring knowledge and beliefs given by others.

After His enlightenment at the age of twenty-one, Osho completed His academic studies and spent several years teaching philosophy at the University of Jabalpur. Meanwhile, He travelled throughout India giving talks, challenging orthodox religious leaders in public debate questioning traditional beliefs, and meeting people from all walks of life. He read extensively, everything He could find to broaden His understanding of the belief systems and psychology of contemporary man. By the late 1960's Osho had begun to develop His unique dynamic meditation techniques. Modern man, He said, is so burdened with the outmoded traditions of the past and the anxieties of modern-day living that he must go through a deep cleansing process before he can hope to discover the thought-less, relaxed state of meditation.

In the early 1970's, the first Westerners began to hear of Osho. By 1974 a commune had been established around Him in Poona, India, and the trickle of visitors from the West was soon to become a flood. In the course of His work, Osho has spoken on virtually every aspect of the development of human consciousness. He has distilled the essence of what is significant to the spiritual quest of contemporary man, based not on intellectual understanding but tested against His own existential experience.

He belongs to no tradition — "I am the beginning of a totally new religious consciousness," He says. "Please don't connect me with the past — it is not even worth remembering."

His talks to disciples and seekers from all over the world have been published in more than six hundred volumes, and translated into over thirty languages.

Osho left His body on January 19, 1990, as a result of poisoning by US government agents while held incognito in custody on technical immigration violations in 1985. His huge Commune in India continues to be the largest spiritual growth centre in the world, attracting thousands of international visitors who come to participate in its meditation, therapy, bodywork and creative programs, or just to experience being in a buddhafield.

for further information about Osho contact

OSHO COMMUNE INTERNATIONAL
17, KOREGAON PARK, PUNE-1, MS, INDIA.
PH. 0212-628562, FAX: 0212 624181
E-mail: cc.osho @ oci.sprintrpg.ems.vsnl.net.in
Internet WEB site: http://www.osho.org

BOOKS BY OSHO

ENGLISH LANGUAGE EDITIONS

EARLY DISCOURSES AND WRITINGS
A Cup of Tea
Dimensions Beyond The Known
From Sex to Superconsciousness
The Great Challenge
Hidden Mysteries
I Am The Gate
Psychology of the Esoteric
Seeds of Wisdom

MEDITATION
And Now and Here (Vol 1 & 2)
In Search of the Miraculous (Vol 1 & 2)
Meditation: The Art of Ecstasy
Meditation: The First and Last Freedom
Vigyan Bhairav Tantra
 (boxed 2-volume set with 112 meditation
 cards)
Yaa-Hoo! The Mystic Rose

BUDDHA AND BUDDHIST MASTERS
The Dhammapada (Vol 1-12)
 The Way of the Buddha
The Diamond Sutra
The Discipline of Transcendence (Vol 1)
The Discipline of Transcendence (Vol 2-4)
The Heart Sutra The Book of Wisdom
 (combined edition of Vol 1 & 2)

BAUL MYSTICS
The Beloved (Vol 1 & 2)

KABIR
The Divine Melody
Ecstasy: The Forgotten Language
The Fist in the Sea is Not Thirsty
The Great Secret
The Guest
The Path of Love
The Revolution

JESUS AND CHRISTIAN MYSTICS
Come Follow to You (Vol 1-4)
I Say Unto You (Vol 1 & 2)
The Mustard Seed
Theologia Mystica

JEWISH MYSTICS
The Art of Dying
The True Sage

SUFISM
Just Like That
Journey to the Heart (same as Until You Die)
The Perfect Master (Vol 1 & 2)
The Secret
Sufis: The Peole of the Path (Vol 1 & 2)
Unio Mystica (Vol 1 & 2)
The Wisdom of the Sands (Vol 1 & 2)

TANTRA
Tantra: The Supreme Understanding
The Tantra Experience The Royal Song of
 Saraha (same as Tantra Vision, Vol 1)
The Tantric Transformation The Royal Song
 of Saraha (same as Tantra Vision, Vol 2)
Book of the Secrets (Vol 4)

TAO
The Empty Boat
The Secret of Secrets
Tao: The Golden Gate
Tao: The Pathless Path
Tao: The Three Treasures
When the Shoe Fits

THE UPANISHADS
Heartbeat of the Absolute Ishavasya
 Upanishad
I Am That Isa Upanishad
Philosophia Ultima Mandukya Upanishad
The Supreme Doctrine Kenopanishad
Finger Pointing to the Moon Adhyatma
 Upanishad
That Art Thou Sarvasar Upanishad, Kaivalya
 Upanishad, Adhyatma Upanishad
The Ultimate Alchemy Atma Pooja Upanishad
 (Vol 1 & 2)
Vedanta: Seven Steps to Samadhi Akshaya
 Upanishad
Behind A Thousand Names Nirvana
 Upanishad

WESTERN MYSTICS
Guida Spirituale *On the Desiderata*
The Hidden Harmony *The Fragments of Heraclitus*
The Messiah (Vol 1 & 2)
  Commentaries on Khalil Gibran's The Prophet
The New Alchemy: To Turn You On
  Commentaries on Mabel Collins' Light on the Path
Philosophia Perennis (Vol 1 & 2)
  The Golden Verses of Pythagoras
Zarathustra: A God That Can dance
Zarathustra: The Laughing Prophet
  Commentaries on Nietzsche's Thus Spake Zarathustra

YOGA
Yoga: The Alpha and the Omega (Vol 1-10)
Yoga: The Science of the Soul (Vol 1-3)
  (same as Yoga: The Alpha and the Omega, Vol 1-3)

ZEN AND ZEN MASTERS
Ah, This!
Ancient Music in the Pines
And the Flowers Showered
A Bird on the Wing (same as Roots and Wings)
Bodhidharma: The Greatest Zen Master
Communism and Zen Fire, Zen Wind
Dang Dang Doko Dang
The First Principle
God is Dead: Now Zen is the Only Living Truth
The Grasss Grows By Itself
The Great Zen Master Ta Hui
Hsin Hsin Ming: The Book of Nothing
  Discourses on the Faith-Mind of Sosan
I Celebrate Myself: God is No Where, Life is Now Here
Kyozan: A True Man of Zen
Nirvana: The Last Nightmare
No Mind: The Flowers of Eternity
No Water, No Moon
One Seed Makes the Whole Earth Green
Returning to the Source
The Search: Talks on the 10 Bulls of Zen
A Sudden Clash of Thunder
The Sun Rises in the Evening
Take it Easy (Vol 1) *Poems of Ikkyu*
Take it EAsy (Vol 2) *Poems of Ikkyu*
This Very Body the Buddha *Hakuin's Song of Meditation*
Walking in Zen, Sitting in Zen
The White Lotus,
Yakusan: Straight to the Point of Enlightenment
Zen Manifesto: Freedom From Oneself
Zen: The Mystery and the Poetry of the Beyond

Zen: The Path of Paradox (Vol 1, 2 & 3)
Zen: The Special Transmission

ZEN BOXED SETS
The World of Zen (5 volumes)
Live Zen
This. This. A Thousand Times This
Zen: The Diamond Thunderbolt
Zen: The Quantum Leap from Mind to No-Mind
Zen: The Solitary Bird, Cuckoo of the Forest
Zen: All The Colors of The Rainbow (5 volumes)
The Buddha: The Emptiness of the Heart
The Language of Existence
The Miracle
The Original Man
Turning in

Osho: On the Ancient Masters of Zen (7 voumes)
Dogen: The Zen Master
Hyakujo: The Everest of Zen—With Basho's haikus
Isan: No Footprints in the Blue Sky
Joshu: The Lion's Roar
Ma Tzu: The Empty Mirror
Nansen: The Point of Departure
Rinzai: Master of the Irrational
* Each volume is also available individually

RESPONSES TO QUESTIONS
Be Still and Know
Come, Come, Yet Again Come
The Goose is Out
The Great Pilgrimage: From Here to Here
The Invitation
My Way: The Way of the White Clouds
Nowhere to Go But In
The Razor's Edge
Walk Without Feet, Fly Without Wings
  and Think Without Mind
The Wild Geese and the Water
Zen: Zest, Zip, Zap and Zing

TALKS IN AMERICA
From Bondage to Freedom
Frion Darkness to Light
From Death to Deathlessness
From the False to the Truth
From Unconsciousness to Consciousness
The Rajneesh Bible (Vol 2-4)
The Rajneesh Upanishad

THE WORLD TOUR
Beyond Enlightenment *Talks in Bombay*
Beyond Psychology *Talks in Uruguay*
Light on the Path *Talks in the Himalayas*
The Path of the Mystic *Talks in Uruguay*
Sermons in Stones *Talks in Bombay*
Socrates Poisoned Again After 25 Centuries
  Talks in Greece

The Sword and the Lotus *Talks in the Himalaya*
The Transmission of the Lamp *Talks in Uruguay*

OSHO'S VISION FOR THE WORLD
The Golden Future
The Hidden Splendor
The New Dawn
The Rebel
The Rebellious Spirit

THE MANTRA SERIES
Hari Om Tat Sat
Om Mani Padme Hum
Om Shantih Shantih Shantih
Sat-Chit-Anand
Satyam-Shivam-Sundaram

PERSONAL GLIMPSES
Books I Have Loved
Glimpses of a Golden Childhood
Notes of a Madman

INTERVIEWS WITH THE WORLD PRESS
The Last Testament (Vol 1)

INTIMATE TALKS BETWEEN MASTER AND DISCIPLE—DARSHAN DIARIES
A Rose is a Rose is a Rose
Be Realistic: Plan for a Miracle
Believing the Impossible Before Breakfast
Beloved of My Heart
Blessed of My Heart
Blessed are the Ignorant
Dance Your Way to God
Don't Just Do Something, Sit There
Far Beyond the Stars
For Madmen Only (Price of Admission: Your Mind)
The Further Shore
Get Out of Your Own Way
God's Got A Thing about You
God is Not for Sale
The Great Nothing
Hallelujah!
Let Go!
The 99 Names of Nothingness
No Book, No Buddha, No Teaching, No Disciple
Nothing to Lose but Your Head
Only Losers Can Win in This Game
Open Door
Open Secret

The Shadow of the Whip
The Sound of One Hand Clapping
The Sun Behind the Sun Behind the Sun
The Tongue-Tip Taste of Tao
This Is It
Turn On, Tune In and Drop the Lot
What Is, Is, What Ain't, Ain't
Won't You Join The Dance

COMPILATIONS
Bhagwan Shree Rajneesh: On Basic Human Rights
Jesus Crucified Again, This Time in Ronald Reagan's America
Priests and Politicians: The Mafia of the Soul

GIFT BOOKS OF OSHO QUOTATIONS
A Must for Contemplation Before Sleep
A Must for Morning Contemplation
Gold Nuggets
More Gold Nuggets
Words From a Man of No Words
At the Feet of the Master

PHOTOBOOKS
Shree Rajneesh: A Man of Many Climates, Seasons and Rainbows *through the eye of the camera*
Impression... *Osho Commune International Photobook*

Books About Osho
Bhagwan: The Buddha for the Future
by *Juliet Forman, S.R.N., S.C.M., R.M.N.*
Bhagwan Shree Rajneesh: The Most Dangerous Man Since Jesus Christ *by Sue Appleton, LL.B., M.A.B.A.*
Bhagwan: The Most Godless Yet the Most Godly Man *by Dr. George Meredith, M.D., M.B.B.S., M.R.C.P.*
Bhagwan: One Man Agianst the Whole Ugly Past of Humanity *by Juliet Forman, S.R.N., S.C.M., R.M.N.*
Bhagwan: Twelve Days That Shook the World *by Juliet Forman, S.R.N., S.C.M., R.M.N.*
Was Bhagwan Shree Rajneesh Poisoned by Ronald Reagan's America? *by Sue Appleton, LL.B. M.A. B.A.*
Diamond Days With Osho
by *Ma Prem Shunyo*

GIFTS
Zorba the Buddha Cookbook

for Osho books, audio/video tapes contact
SADHANA FOUNDATION
17, KOREGAON PARK, PUNE-1, MS, INDIA
PH: 0212-628562, FAX : 0212-624181